HAR$H AFFAIRS

Book One of the Geralds Saga trilogy

Meg Cartwright

ISBN 978-09919033-1-3

Editors: Rita Vassallo, Mike Sauve

Cover design: Hume Media Inc.

Published by Publishing House VETEMA
Toronto
Printed in Canada

AVAILABLE NOW AT ISELFMALL.COM
Contact   iself.org@gmail.com   for order information

This book is dedicated to all the people who suffer from depression.

I want to thank my very smart and charming daughters Vesi and Tsvetty for their help.

This book would not have been possible without the support and encouragement of my friend Dhakshi Kumar

TABLE OF CONTENTS

PART ONE

ROBERT

CHAPTER ONE

The ruthless buzz of my new cell phone woke me up this morning. It's a new model. Actually the latest to hit the market and is no bigger than a child's palm. Fancy. Exquisite. A real gem of contemporary technology. The display said it was 10:30 but there was no caller ID.

"Hello!" I said, trying to sound brisk. I didn't get the desired effect. No matter how hard I tried, my voice still sounded like a husky barking dog.

"Robert? I'm in the office. Are you still in bed? For God's sake. Don't you think you should be in the office by now?"

To my deepest regret it was my boss, Elliott.

How on earth!

He wasn't due back from a conference in Chicago until tomorrow. So what he was doing in the office?

Not once, in all the years we've known each other had out-smarted this guy. My first thought was that I had to give him a sound excuse for my absence. But what? If I told him I was dopey, which was exactly the case, I absolutely wouldn't get his sympathy. So I faked exhaustion and said:

"Sorry Elliott, I've got a bit of a frog in my throat. I think I've got a nasty virus. But, whatever. I'll be on my way in a couple of minutes."

My excuse didn't impress him at all, at least not in the way I anticipated. He obviously could tell, without a doubt, the exact reason for my infection. Also, he was pretty much aware of the exact name of "the virus" that had "invited" the frog into my throat.

What followed next was Elliott's chilly discontent. He said:

"Come straight to my office. I want to discuss two extremely important issues with you. It's urgent."

Then the line went dead.

The effect on me was immediate. I was completely awake as his ice-cold voice was a substitute for my morning ritual cold shower. Shaving on the fly and skipping my daily workout, I dashed into my favorite Porsche and practically flew to the Gerald Bank, located on Wall Street in downtown New York.

I do stupid things when I'm drunk. When in an alcoholic bliss, I become overly generous to my staff. Last night, just before dawn, when my driver brought me up to my room, instead of hitting the bed right away, in an outburst of drunkard's enthusiasm, I released him for the whole day. Now, he's most likely lying in the arms of his mistress, without the slightest intention to work today... unlike me.

I definitely needed some rest myself after such a crazy night. It would've been a nice day off with my boss out of town. But no way. He had to show up two days earlier. And now the shitty city traffic was making my head spin. I somehow made my way to the bank safe and sound. I stopped my car in front of the main entrance.

The building looked almost the same as it did when the original owner, our great-grandfather, Daniel Gerald, died and left it to his heirs. The facade went through a few renovations through the years and the some of the old stylish furniture originally found in the lobby was restored or moved elsewhere. The changes made to the building were mostly cosmetic. Instead of modernizing the building, Management chose to spend a fortune on highly sophisticated office and bank equipment.

* * *

Our great-grandfather *found his initial fortune in real estate. Then he invested the money into a couple of high profile civil engineering projects. When things finally went well, he married a rich heiress for convenience, and ultimately opened a bank.*

But the bank really went big when my grandfather, Robert Gerald, led the company. He paved the way towards the bank's present prosperity.

The bank now provides a full range of financial and investment management services, and has branches in 50 states and a worldwide presence. Gerald Bank has consistently been ranked by Fortune magazine as one of America's 50 Most Admired Companies.

Grandpa Robert had five children - my father, Ted; my uncle and current President, Elliott; two other uncles - Ben and Oliver; and my aunt, Melanie. I was the first of the youngest generation to work for the family business, right after obtaining my MBA from Harvard three years ago. Of course I started at entry level. But when you're family, one gets promoted quite quickly. So here I am, three years later, a VP of Gerald Bank. It's a nice cushy life with many perks and privileges - a secretary, driver, company car, and personal assistant, not to mention stock incentives. Not bad for a 29 year old, huh?

* * *

I threw the keys to the door-keeper to park my car, nodded to the security guards and dashed through the lobby straight to the elevators. The CEO's office was on the third floor.

Mrs. Florence Mason, Elliott's secretary, welcomed me with a smile as I rushed in. She was in her late thirties, but looked younger. When she came back from Elliott's office and approached me, I could smell her brand-name, expensive perfume that could possibly inspire passion and desire in a lot of men, but for me it was just a fragrance. I'm not a great fan of brunettes. So even though I recognized the charm and charisma of this stylish woman, I thought of her only as a professional, one that I could only show respect to.

I made my way to the door to meet with my "favorite" uncle who I was sure was waiting for me impatiently. The moment I entered the room and saw him, I again felt shivers of mortal fear creeping up my spine. Nobody would know that being around him gives me a weird feeling. I'm his "right hand" and everyone in the banking business knows it.

* * *

The office of the CEO had not changed much since my grandfather's time: The pictures on the walls were hung on first day Daniel Gerald moved in, and the books in the huge bookcase looked as if the old banker had just set them up - his favorite passtime at the end of the heavy working week. The things that Elliott dared to change in the office were changed out of necessity: ergonomic furniture in the meeting room and up-to-date office equipment to suit the most senior position in the firm.

* * *

Elliott was working on his computer with a look of concentration. But when I came closer I saw that he was playing one of his favorite games. The game's rules allow players to run it endlessly, only the complete destruction of a rival player will end the game. He always played this game when facing a serious problem. I knew how ambitious he was and instinctively shuddered at the thought that today I might completely replace his computer rival, but in real life.

Elliott is a good looking man in his late forties. He had a body that was well built for his age, a sophisticated and sharp face, and it was no secret that he was very intelligent as well. He has a typical Gerald's look: blond hair, gray eyes and very light skin. Every family member is blonde excluding my father Ted and I. We both have very dark hair and eyes. Our skin colour is also much darker in comparison to the others. We're like two black swans in a flock of white ones.

"Take a seat, Robert," he said with his head still down gazing at the screen.

I almost collapsed on one of the chairs in the meeting room.

Oh yes, I was so frustrated.

We stayed silent for a couple of minutes while Elliott kept on moving his mouse on the pad. I waited and waited, every second of silence making me more nervous. When I lost my patience and decided to break the silence, Elliott stopped clicking and sharply rolled away from the computer desk. Just like a mischievous kid, he rolled into the meeting room on his chair, legs up high in the air.

I was already waiting for him like a cat on hot bricks. Finally we were already facing each other and he was staring at me with a cold glare that made me feel like he was cutting me apart.

"May I ask where you were last night?"

It didn't make any sense to hide. The real question I was being asked was "Where did you go to get drunk?"

"At Marco's club. I meet my former classmates on regular basis there. It's not about the drinking. It's mostly, you know, networking, friendship and sharing ideas."

"Especially when you know I'm out of town? You were planning on taking the day off weren't you?"

It was stupid to deny it.

"I want you to stop partying and drinking during the week and to be here on time, every morning. You know the unofficial company policy in regards to sick days, days off and delays, right?"

"Yes, sir."

There wasn't any trust in his voice when he continued:

"The rules are for all employees and especially for the company owners who are expected to be good role models for the others to follow. Do you have anything to say?"

"No, sir."

"No? Are you sure? I'm assuming no alcohol abuse problems again?"

"You know the reason for that but I overcame it, Elliott."

"Yeah, this bitch. I know. Alright. Let's get to the topic at hand then."

I froze.

He started talking quietly and slowly:

"I had a meeting with a very important client."

I heaved a sigh of relief. It was not the usual set-up that he ruthlessly used to provoke me.

I felt like a fool. I thought that something horrible had happened, something crucial and fatal. He'd outsmarted me again. Yes, he was just playing the "big boss" game to keep me alert, to be in "good shape" as he used to say.

I hated him because of those little, dirty games and lousy tricks that he obviously played with the greatest of pleasure.

"Yes?" I immediately put on an interested expression, trying to hide the relief that I still couldn't quickly conceal.

"I want you to make a small investigation before I give a copy of this extremely important offer to the shareholders."

"Which company are you talking about?"

"These are the papers. Take a look," he handed me a binder without any sign that he noticed my nervousness. Maybe I was being too touchy.

"The company management is very close to the government of one Middle Eastern country."

"Don't say that...the Middle East? Right now, they are undergoing much turmoil."

"Yes, exactly, it is the Middle Eastern country," he stressed.

"You must be crazy. It is in a war all the time, don't you know that? Every single day they fight - with us, with the Palestinians, with the Jews. Nobody knows when exactly the country will start another war."

I opened the binder and took a glance of the first page.

"War? So what?"

"So what? If a new war comes-up? This part of the world had always been a dormant volcano ready to explode. Do you remember the Balkans? What happened with our transactions during the war in Afghanistan?"

"I don't care about the war. Our dilemma is whether the company we are considering partnering with is conducting a legitimate business or operating in the grey economy."

"Okay."

"All its activities and transactions look fine at first glance. But I'm suspicious about how they win all those tenders, organized by the government authorities. Corruption? Bribes? I want to know everything about those tenders - participants, offers, subcontractors, best bidders. Understand? Everything."

"You have never objected to the origin of money so far, have you?"

"No I didn't. I don't care now either. I need to get the clear picture of how the company is managed in case we go further with these guys and enter into business with them."

He jumped up and approached the window. Something grabbed his attention outside and it seemed as if he forgot about me and our conversation.

Just as I thought our conversation was over and I could take a breath Elliott spoke:

"Are you going out with my daughter?"

Indeed, I was told that he wanted to talk about two issues. We had finished with the first less important issue, now he turned his attention to the main issue.

I jumped from the chair and instantly found myself in front of him.

I was almost two heads taller than him.

He was not a large man - he was fine boned and from the back he looked almost like a boy.

I stood in front of him and looked directly at his delicate face and the coldest grey eyes that I have ever seen.

"With Lucy? Yeah. We are just hanging out, you know."

"No dating?"

"Dating? But she's a kid, man. You must be kidding me."

"Not at all. I'm completely serious. My bodyguards are telling me a different story and let me tell you, Lucy is not a kid anymore. The only problem here is that she's your cousin."

"I don't understand. There is nothing between us, just…"

"I don't think it's a good idea to continue going out with her. You know that I don't like dirty, stupid games."

"What do you mean by "dirty games"?"

"Trying to seduce Lucy. She's not an ordinary girl. Never forget that."

"I know, but…"

"So you want her money? Stop this game right now."

"I'm not playing any games and I'm not seducing her. You cannot stop us from seeing each other."

"I'm her father so I'm going to do what's best for her. And what's best for her is for you two to stop seeing each other. Did I make myself clear?"

"Yes, sir."

He looked at me and his eyes seemed to scan my soul.

"You can go now. And keep me posted on the deal."

I wish I slammed the door but instead I closed it silently.

Mrs. Florence Mason saw my face, even though she certainly didn't know about the second part of our conversation, her eyes seemed to be full of sympathy. Her eyes followed me as I left the office.

"Have a nice day," she said quietly, but I didn't answer.

I wanted to go to my office upstairs.

I was walking as if I was in a dream and I didn't take the stairs as usual. I stood in front of the elevators looking like a zombie. The door opened, I got in and threw a glance at the mirror on the wall. What I saw was a man in his late twenties, dressed in an expensive suit and elegant tie. I looked into the eyes of this apparently prosperous, successful businessman and what I saw was enormous anger and disgust.

As I got off the elevator I realised I was on the wrong floor. Mark, the manager of the tellers, greeted me:

"Hi, Robert," he said.

As he was coming towards me to talk business, he gave orders to someone on his phone.

"Anthony, do not buy more yen. For God's sake, man, don't purchase yet."

I could not concentrate on business.

I needed to speak to Lucy.

Before he could stop me, I waived him away and headed towards the stairs.

* * *

I needed to hear Lucy's voice.

How could Elliott say that I'm seducing her because of his money? I still couldn't believe he'd said that.

He was right about one thing: I like Lucy.

I don't care about Elliott's plans and dirty games. I don't want his money.

I only want his daughter.

My cousin!

God, help me!

* * *

"It's me, kiddo," I told her when she picked up the phone. "Are you at school?"

"Yeah, but it's lunch time so we can talk."

"I would like to see you tonight. Are you busy?"

"What's wrong? Your voice sounds strange."

"I can't tell you over the phone."

"I have a test tomorrow and a project due, so I need to study.

16

Is it something important?"

"Not at all. Good luck on your test tomorrow. Give me a call when you have a chance."

"Sure. Everything alright?"

"Yes, yes, focus on your studies."

"Okay then, talk to ya soon."

CHAPTER TWO

I **did everything possible** to leave at five, but it was a busy day.

A number of clients came to the office unexpectedly to talk to me. I dictated a couple of important letters and gave instructions to my secretary to send several e-mails. At the last minute I Skyped a regular client located in Atlanta and we talked for a long time about his portfolio.

It was already quite dark outside when I finally left the office. I was planning to finish earlier, but when I arrived at the entrance to my building, the clock said nine. The front door automatically opened and the concierge told me:

"Good evening, Mr. Gerald. Sir, a young girl is waiting for you in the lobby."

I was still lost in my thoughts and looked at him astonished, but before he could explain more, I heard a very familiar voice:

"Bobby."

When I turned around to see where the voice was coming from, I saw Lucy in the lobby coming towards me.

She was wearing sweatpants, a hoody and really ugly Ugg boots and listening to music on her cell. She looked like any other teen in the city. As her father said in the morning, she was not an ordinary girl but here and now, I could see only a teen and nothing else.

Did that crazy man tell her already?

* * *

Lucy is almost eleven years younger *than I am and I have always considered her as a person from another generation. We didn't spend a lot of time together as kids and I hadn't seen her at all while I attended Harvard. I only met her again at Edward's premiere on Broadway four months ago. Edward is our cousin and the most famous person in the family. He is an actor and a famous movie star.*

The premiere was his first performance on a Broadway stage. It was an occasion to celebrate, and the whole family attended.

Before the play, in the foyer of the theatre, I met Elliott and his wife Pamela with a girl that I barely recognized as Lucy. She used to be a cute kid and now she was an attractive teenager.

She looked hot - exactly my type: long blond hair, long legs and well-shaped boobs. The strapless green dress she wore matched the color of her almond-shaped emerald eyes. The dress, short and provocative was low cut and looking at her made my head feel dizzy.

We didn't have time to speak because the play was about to start. However, at the special dinner party after the show, I had a chance to talk to her, as we happened to be at the same table.

"How's school?" I asked.

"Going well. Almost done."

"You're graduating this year, right?"

"In June."

"Great. I don't think you're studying all the time. What do you like to do for fun?"

"Oh, a lot of stuff. Sports, watching movies. I'm also modeling."

"I can see that you would be successful as a model. You look breath-taking."

She looked at me with interest.

"Thanks, cousin. What do you do for fun?"

"Well, hang out with friends, go to the gym, I'm a busy guy."

After the dessert, I asked her:

"You want to dance?"

"Yeah. I'd love to."

She was a good dancer and I was sorry when the music stopped and she said:

"I'm thirsty. Let's go to the bar and get some refreshments."

"Okay," I said, and then we heard a voice behind us:

"Oh, my favourite cousins!"

We both turned.

It was Edward.

* * *

From a young age Edward was a creative person: playing roles, coming up with different stories and performing them.

His dream was to study acting
Deviations from the family rules never worked out well.

Edward isn't an exception. He was pushed towards the traditional career path and went to study at Harvard. After enormous, painful efforts, he graduated from the MBA Program, as every Gerald did.

But instead of joining the bank, like the rest of us, he went to Hollywood. There he entered the movie industry and started playing small roles on TV. He became famous after starring in a television series, some soap operas and films. His fame reached New York, not only as a movie star but also as one of the most popular bohemians. Then my crazy cousin came back to New York because he was doing a play in a Broadway theater.

Eddy had left the home of his conservative parents, Oliver and Kimberly Gerald, a large mansion near New York, and now he was living in one wonderful studio next to Broadway.

Eddy's father, Oliver Gerald, is another member of our family who has a reason to hate Elliott.

He continues to work for the bank, but his status as an Executive Vice President will be the peak of his career. When his father reorganized the bank Oliver was not promoted. Instead, he now reports to his younger brother. He lives with this humiliation and disappointment every day. His son is another disappointment, as Oliver considers acting as an activity for losers.

Edward was living in his own world, the world of acting. Bank operations, money transfers, and financial transactions were just boring activities for him. He was interested in money just to secure a luxurious life for himself and to be able to host extravagant, costly parties for his friends.

He referred clients to the bank--people in the entertainment industry with projects that needed financing. When the bank financed these projects, Edward received commissions. These referrals were his only contribution to the family business.

* * *

Edward looks much younger than his thirty-one years. Blond, tall and well built, he wears expensive, brand name clothes designed to look, unpretentious and casual. With the boyish smile of a kind, naive, teenager, he is charming and glamorous. His appearance however is deceiving. Hollywood's games are no less brutal than Wall Street's deals and only the strongest and most dedicated players can survive. If you look closely you will find the stubborn mouth and strong hard jaw of a man capable of being one of the survivors. Obviously, such a shark jaw was necessary in Hollywood.

* * *

"**Thanks, guys**, for coming. It is so nice to see you here tonight."
Lucy hugged him.
"Eddy, you're amazing! I'm so proud of you!"
"Thanks, sweety."
"I cannot believe I'm hugging a real movie star. I'm sorry, Eddy, if I'm annoying. Don't your fans drive you crazy?"
"Oh, let me tell ya. Robert, I need to talk to you about one my new projects as a producer. I want to put some money into a business-oriented reality show. My new girlfriend is a television journalist and the host of a business program. I need your professional advice on some issues."
"Sounds interesting. Call me so we can talk."
"I enrolled in The UCLA School of Theatre, Film, and Television and established my own company Gerald Productions. I want to talk about that project too."
"Okay. Not a problem. You did a lot of stuff, bro."
Lucy looked bored. She interrupted me.
"Come on, boys. You can speak about business later. Robert, here is my cell. Can you take a picture of us? I want to post it on my Facebook. Do you want to join, Robert? Come here with us. I'll take a picture of the three of us. Okay, I'll download them now."
"Oh, look who's here," said Eddy.
I looked behind me and saw Tom Arkwright, one of my classmates at Harvard. He was backing some of Eddy's projects. We looked at each other with a tension. His lips curved in a restrained smile, but his eyes remained cold blue.
"Good evening, Robert."
"Hi Tom."
"Tom, you know our cousin Lucy, right?" asked Eddy.
"No," said Tom. "I never had that pleasure."

"Really?" Eddy was surprised. "But I clearly remember you met her at my birthday party. Oh, it was Cassidy, my other cousin, of course. Well then, let me introduce you to my cousin Lucy. She is graduating from high school this year. Lucy, this is Tom Arkwright, a banker and one of my business partners."

"How are you, Lucy," Tom said kindly, putting on his restrained smile again while handing out his hand.

"I'm doing fine. Thanks. How are you?"

"Oh, I'm excited. Enjoying the show and this awesome party."

"I'm going to grab another drink, guys. I'll be right back," said Eddy.

"I'll come with you to get some juice," said Lucy. We'll be back in a minute, Robert."

Tom and I stayed put.

The tension between us was hanging in the air.

He broke the silence first.

"I heard you have been promoted to VP, Robert. Congrats."

"Thanks. How are things with you?"

"Not too bad. Let's hope that after the last election's results became known, the market will get out of this crisis. I'm starting to get tired of the politicians' games."

"As far as I know, you have a special role in these games."

"Well, strong words. My games are quite little."

"Are you sure?"

"Robert, will you ever forgive me?"

"Would you forgive someone who steals the girl you love and then throws her away like she's a piece of garbage?"

He didn't answer and continued to stare at me silently, but the pride in his eyes was gone.

Just in time, Eddy and Lucy came back.

"Ok, I'm going to see where my partner is and I'll talk to you later, Eddy. Lucy, it was pleasure meeting you and I hope to see you again. Maybe we can go out for a drink some time."

In that moment, I realized I wanted her for myself.

"I'm not sure if that's a good idea," I interrupted him rudely.

"I understand. I'll be on my way then."

He turned to me and we stood and stared at each other with resentment.

23

The memories went back to Harvard and our friendship. He cheated, not me.

I hated him and couldn't forgive him. He hated me because I would not give him my forgiveness.

It was not the pain associated with him stealing my girlfriend - that pain had already gone away, nor was it that they both had betrayed me that kept me from forgiving him. It was that I had lost the hope that I could ever trust anyone again.

It was then that I started drinking again.

"Bye, Robert. It was a pleasure to see you."

I didn't answer.

At that moment, an attractive reporter from People magazine asked Eddy for a short interview and they both left. I asked Lucy to have another dance.

"Why do you hate that guy?" Lucy asked, and I was surprised at how observant she was.

"Was it that obvious?"

"Yeah, it was all because of some girl, right? Your girlfriend?"

I started laughing.

"I'm impressed, Lucy. Yes, you are right, it was about a girl, my girlfriend."

"Do you still love her?"

It took me a minute before I answered.

"I don't think so."

"Is she still with him? Just curious."

"No. He left her after a month."

"Wow! You still suffer from that, don't you?"

It took me another minute before I answered.

"It was three years ago and the fact that she chose him was painful but now it's just part of the past. I have to move forward."

"Yeah, definitely." Lucy agreed.

I looked at her eyes and said:

"I just met a girl, my cousin actually, that could help me. Do you want to?"

She gave me the sweetest smile in the world.

"Yes, I do."

Since that night, we have been seeing each other. We didn't know if there was anything between us. We never clarified our relationship. The only thing we knew was that we enjoyed being around each other.

When Elliott ordered me to stop seeing Lucy, I realized I was willing to kill everyone who wanted to separate us.

* * *

"**Lucy! My God!** What are you doing here so late?"
We hugged.
"Hey, Bobby. I need to talk to you."
"What's up?"
"Not much, but I need your help."
"Sure. Let's go to my apartment. "
My apartment is on the top floor of a new modern condo building. I love the beautiful views that reveal the city and the distant towers of Manhattan. At night, the view is amazing. The condo is open concept, with small and ergonomic furniture. I hired a Puerto Rican couple to take care of my bachelor abode. I prefer the servants and the driver not to interact with me and have rented rooms for them in the same building, which is convenient becouse although they do not live in they're always at hand.

My favorite place is my sunroom where I like to surf the net or read magazines on the developments in high technology. From the window on one side of the sofa-bed I can access the roof terrace, where in the summer I love to drink my coffee and drinks.

When we entered the apartment I realized how hungry I was.
"Did you tell your mom that you are at my place?"
"I sent her a message."
"Text her that I'll drive you home. Do it now while I check if dinner is ready. I'll be right back."
"It's okay. I'm not hungry."
I'm starving. Just keep me company."
" Alright."
"Are you prepared for tomorrow?" I asked when I returned.
"I hope so."
"The mid-term is just around the corner, right?
"Yeah."
We settled down in the dining room.
"Some wine?"

"You know I'm not allowed to drink."

"It's tender Italian wine."

"Bobby, you're so cute. Ok, just a sip and don't tell my Dad."

"Melissa, can you get utensils for Lucy, please," I asked the housekeeper who was serving dinner.

"Si, sir" said Melissa.

I love her Spanish accent.

"Do you want some stewed veal? Melissa is a magician in the kitchen. You need to try it," I said after the housekeeper put the utensils in front of her.

"Oh, I could not eat a morsel. She looked like a fastidious child who refuses to eat breakfast and drink milk, but then she hesitated and finally changed her mind.

"Well, well, I smell something very yummy," she said like a small, capricious kid. "Actually I haven't eaten since this morning and my stomach has twisted into a ball."

Melissa also brought other delicacies and drinks.

"Do you want some crayfish in the marinade? You will find that this is the best appetizer for our wine."

"Oh Crabs! I love them."

"Try Melissa's breaded chicken nuggets."

"How can I resist these delicious meals? You're such a gourmet."

"Unfortunately I don't have so much time for that. Now listen and follow my instructions: eat some fried morsels, add a little feta cheese. So...come on, now slowly, have a drink, a sip of wine. Slowly. You can feel it. Good. Take a breath. How do you smell that?"

She was following my instructions diligently.

"Mmm…. Awesome!"

Once she'd discovered the secrets of wine tasting, we had to focus on her problems. I waited so she could experience the pleasure of good food and drink before we got to the point:

"And now, after having enjoyed this pleasant part of life tell me what's going on?"

She answered me directly, without hesitating for a moment:

"I don't want to live with my parents anymore. I have serious problems at home."

"Why? What happened?"

I didn't know what to think. Did Elliott tell her something about us or was it something else?

"I just have to leave, Robert."

"Speak out, kiddo. What exactly is the problem?"

This time she hesitated, seemed to think, took a slow sip of wine and looked at me over the edge of the glass.

"The problem is that Dad is over-parenting. He doesn't respect me or listen to my opinion. He says "no" to everything I really want. For example, I wanted to start working with an advertising agency as a model.The photographer of this agency met me in a cafe and said that I have the qualities of a model. Well, what do you think my father did? It was a "no" again. My mother thought it was an unprestigious occupation for a girl with high social status."

"When you finish school you will be able to make your own decisions."

"I don't think so. My father is pushing me to go to Harvard as "all the Geralds go to Harvard." Honestly, Bobby, I cannot care less. I want to take Design Management at New York University."

"Of course, it is better to conform to the traditions and go to Harvard, but...."

"Sometimes he says that I can choose, other times he voices the opposite opinion. As if he deliberately wants to annoy me. I think there is a lot of tension in my family lately and I'm not sure if I can survive it."

"Of course you will."

"Well, but you didn't hear everything. You know what just happened? He took my cell phone! Can you imagine? My phone is my life. My friends are there, my Facebook, my everything. At that moment, I felt like he didn't take just my cell, that he took my soul, Robert. Like I'm stupid or insane and not able to make my own decisions."

"Don't blame him, Lucy. Sometimes fathers are quite jealous towards their daughters."

"Jealous? No, he's a dictator. He wants to control me. However, he needs to understand that this is my life and I don't need his advice on how to live it. I told my father that. In addition,

27

I told him if he doesn't trust me, I couldn't trust him either. If you could have seen his expression."

"What about your mom? It seems to me she's very nice and supportive."

"She's kind of. She at least tries to understand me but she always listens to what Dad has to say. She's his shadow."

"Maybe you need to talk to her about how you feel."

"I don't think so. It will be a waste of time. She'll agree with me and then she'll agree with him. I don't want to be like her, not having an opinion."

"She wants all of you to be happy. Ask her to stay on your side."

"I think it will be much easier just to leave and live by myself."

"I don't think it's a good idea to leave your home right now."

"Why are you on their side? I don't get it."

"I'm not. For me it's too early. Finish high school first and then if you decide to stay in New York I promise I'll help you find a condo."

"You know what? I don't want to go home. Can I sleep here on the sofa bed for a while?"

"It's not a problem for me at all, but, as I said, don't do stupid things."

It took me half an hour to convince her to go back home.

* * *

"Did your father say something about me?" I asked her when we were in the car.

"What do you mean, "Something about me"?"

"I mean about us, that we are going out and stuff."

"No, he didn't say anything. Why should he say something? It's not his business."

"Forget it, kiddo. I just asked."

We arrived at her home in silence.

"You are doing the right thing staying with you parents, Lucy. Trust me."

"Have a good night, betrayer."

CHAPTER THREE

The next morning, when the alarm woke me up at 7 a.m., I felt no desire to go to work, but I had no choice.

I rushed with a fake vigour towards my office; with professional courtesy I greeted my administrative assistant and ordered the first coffee of the day. When I was inside my office and the door closed behind me, the apparent enthusiasm disappeared and I relaxed in my chair wearily. I glanced at the newspapers, arranged precisely by my secretary and then asked my executive assistant to come in.

"Coming, Robert," he said over the intercom.

I didn't have to wait long for him. I had just opened my laptop when he knocked on the door. At the same time, a member of the office pool brought a steaming cup of aromatic coffee.

I didn't have even time to say "Come in" when someone opened the door with a flourish and I saw my cousin John. He also graduated from Harvard and is now an Assistant VP. But he will soon be promoted to a VP like me.

He's rather thin, blond haired, with gray eyes and pale face. He has his own unique style in dressing. For example, he is wearing clothes that you would not think go together in terms of colors and textures, but the look is very stylish. Today's outfit is very fancy and although I cannot see myself wearing it, I like it very much.

* * *

Uncle Ben, John's father is the only one who ever dared to challenge Elliott and his method of management and there was an open struggle for control of the bank. It happened three years ago when I was in my last year at Harvard. While completing an internship at the Gerald bank during the summer I heard all about the struggle. Ben was saying the old Gerald had made a mistake choosing Elliott as his successor. He argued loudly that any one of the brothers could manage the bank better than

Elliott, who was getting rid of anyone who was in his way or who was smarter than he was. I was back at Harvard when my Dad called me to tell me that Uncle Ben had a heart attack at his office and died the same day.

Two years later, my father died unexpectedly in plane crash accident. After his death I found a note in his home safe.

It was typed on a computer.

Who wrote it?

Why was this note in my father's safe?

. There was only one thing that was sure. It stated that someone had killed John's father:

"At the bottom of the whole story was this beast. He organized the assassination of Ben. I don't even know why I decided to side with this criminal and why I helped him eliminate Ben, who I actually liked a lot. I convinced myself that I didn't have a choice, but my conscience was not reassuring me. I tried to forget this shameful episode from my past, but it was impossible."

* * *

"What's up, John? How is the research going?" I asked him.

"I' m ready. We can review the information I found." He handed me a folder.

"You did all the research? Very good. It was done quickly."

"I worked on it until 4 a.m., but it's worth it."

"Don't tell me you haven't slept the whole night?"

"A little nap on the couch."

I looked at him.His appearance did not indicate that he had slept in his clothes. He wore a clean, ironed shirt, and suit, and his shoes were shiny. His face looked tired, but shaved. He looked at me and said:

"Do you have another task for me?"

"I'll review the report and call you later."

"Okay, Robert. Are you going to the gym tonight?"

"I need to. I went clubbing with my friends on Tuesday night, so you can imagine what happened."

"You guys are crazy. Did you go to the bar after?"

"Of course. It was the full program. I'll tell you in the gym.

30

Don't want someone to hear us. Especially after "The Old Man" caught me. He said he would be in Chicago for the whole week."

We called Elliott "The Old Man." We were scared even to say his name loudly.

"Oh no. What did he say?"

"Thank God I survived this. I had to listen the usual "lecture". Don't drink, no sick days, bla, bla, bla."

"You should tell him the question is not how much time you spend in the office, It's more important to be effective and productive. The "Old Dragons "are here all day long doing nothing, just talking about golf."

We called our uncles "The Old Dragons." We were scared even to say their names out loud.

"They are our uncles," I said, feigning admonishment.

"I don't care if they are our uncles."

"I'm sure Elliott knows all that, man. Alright, I will talk to you later."

"Okey-dokey. See you at the gym," he said.

* * *

I opened the folder that he had given me and pushed the button on the intercom:

"More coffee, please."

One of my administrative assistants came quickly with a coffee pot.

I continued reading. John had done an excellent job as always. All the information we needed was there, perfectly organized.

I was just about to call Elliott to tell him that the application can be presented to the board when he called me.

"Come to my office immediately, please," he told me with an icy voice and hung up without further explanation.

Elliott was sitting in his swivel chair with the expression of a Sphinx, and I thought: "After yesterday's family quarrels, what triggered his anger this time?"

"I'll ask you straight and I want you to answer me honestly. Why did you tell Lucy that I told you to stop seeing her?"

"I didn't. "

Elliott slid down back in his chair.

"Pamela told me Lucy was with you last night."

"Yes, but I didn't tell her about our conversation. We talked about the problems she has in the family. I'm thinking you and Pamela could be more opened minded and reliable."

"It's not your business what is going on in my own family, okay?"

"I don't want to be a reason for conflict between you two but...."

"I don't intend to discuss my family with you. Try to bring me the information I wanted. The meeting of the board is in four hours."

"The documents are ready to be presented."

"Good job, Robert. Win this project and I'll try to forget about your little dirty games."

"Listen Elliott, I don't like it when you talk to me in this disrespectful way. I'm not playing any games."

He looked surprised by my aggressive voice.

"Give me the papers, please."

* * *

I returned to my office and my stomach was a huge and nasty ball of nerves. I ordered a new cup of coffee. After the conversation with Elliott I felt sufficiently motivated to call Lucy.

"Hey." I said when she picked up the phone."Tell me if I'm calling at a bad time, I just wanted to know how you're doing."

"I'm fine," but she sounded uncertain. "Sorry for last night. All this happened because I was so upset."

"I understand. Everything's fine."

"You're so cute. I wish my father was like you."

"Did you have any problems with him last night?"

"We had an almost friendly conversation. I'm very suspicious."

"Suspicious? What do you mean?"

"I've a feeling someone's reading my accounts on Facebook and Twitter."

"You think they somehow found your passwords?"

"I've a feeling that he or more probably my mom's spying on me."

"That's ridiculous."

"It would not be a problem for my father's hackers."

She was right.

"I think you just worry too much. How was the test?"

"I'm just going there."

"Good luck then. I would like to see you today, but I want to give you time to recover. However, for Saturday night I won't accept any excuses. We need to go and see Eddie's new movie. It will be in the theaters on Friday."

I gave her a phone kiss and hung up in the best frame of mind. I thought at dinner I would give her the Cartier bracelet I had already chosen for her.

I felt inspired. I took the file and gave it to Elliott.

* * *

Mr. Gerald, your mother is on line two," said my secretary Jane.

"Put me through, please."

"Robert! How are you?"

"I'm overwhelmed with work, and you?"

"Thank God, I'm okay. Only my allergies are killing me sometimes."

"What about your hormonal problem. Last time I talked to you you were having some hot flashes during the night."

"Dr. Mark prescribed a homeopathic remedy, a special diet, and a new hormone therapy. I feel better now, but I'm still not very well."

"I'm sure you will feel better soon. It might be good therapy to organize something for fun, don't you think?"

"You are right. Maybe I'll organize a small party, only women - Dorothy, Susan, Cynthia, you know my friends here."

I clearly imagined her sitting next to the pool among her friends, all of them rich and widows like her. She liked to gossip with them while drinking light cocktails and fresh juices.

She is in her late fifties, but is looking very well for her age.

Her body is still slim and elegant, and though her face is no longer as tight and smooth as it was when she was young. She takes excellent care of her appearance and uses whatever money can buy to make her look younger. She does not have many responsibilities other than to think about herself and to have fun.

* * *

She met my father in the Gerald Bank where she was an assistant manager in the Law Department, an intermediate level position with very good prospects for future advancement in the firm. My mom was a graduate of Harvard like my Dad, but she graduated from the law school. Once she married my father she refused to work anymore, left the bank and her business career. Everybody thought that my father would become the head of Gerald Bank and that my dear mom had hit the jackpot. When I was born she decided that she had done her duty.

"Ted, I've fulfilled my duty. You're the firstborn son of Robert Gerald, and you now are holding in your hands the future president of the Gerald Bank," she had said.

"I think so, dear," replied my father.

"I plan to name the baby Robert after his grandfather. Robert Gerald."

"That's great, Samantha," my father agreed.

My mother was sure that my birth had finally cemented our branch of the family's position in the family business. She refused to breastfeed me, hired a nurse and nanny to take care of me and started living her own life. Her job was done. Although she was selfish and lazy she did require Dad and I to work hard.

I just turned twenty when my grandfather died.

He was still young and energetic. The sixties are very fruitful for many men. He was thinking about retiring from the bank. He was involved behind the scenes in politics, and was planning to run for office, but fate decided otherwise. The cause of his death was a rare type of cancer that killed him months after he was diagnosed.

The family was very surprised when he appointed his youngest son, Elliott, to the position of bank president.

When it was announced my mother nearly lost her mind. I can still hear her clearly yelling at Dad: "You didn't get the trust of your father.

34

You're without any ambition, so I cannot count on you now or in the future."

But she was wrong.

Now, I know the reason for that decision.

* * *

When I started working at the Gerald Bank, I decided to leave the family mansion, which is located next to Central Park West, and bought my own condo. One year later my Dad died in plane crash. Mom sold the house for $30 million and moved to Santa Monica. She bought an exquisite and luxurious house on the beach.

* * *

"**Are you seeing anyone?** You know I am not the kind of mother who is dying for grandchildren, just asking."

I thought about Lucy.

"Nobody special. I don't have time for dating."

"I'm not pushing you, no rush, no pressure."

"Thanks for that, mom."

There was a silence for a second.

"Are you sure there is no one, your voice sounds different."

"Nothing serious."

"Are you coming for my birthday?" she said, changing the topic.

"I don't know yet. I'll do my best to come. As soon as my schedule is confirmed, I'll let you know."

"Okay then. Call me when you can."

* * *

Today I expected the final report on the project in Middle East. During the negotiations, especially the business lunch with a representative of our potential partner in the transaction I got the impression that the decision would be in our favor. I could not be sure until the last minute because usually such negotiations were held with other investors as well. Based on the data I was given by

John, I thought that we had presented the best offer.

Although I was almost convinced of our success, I waited on tenterhooks to receive the confirmation call. In our business, a deal is not a sure thing until you see the signed contract.

"Mr. Harvey, on the second line," my administrative assistant informed me.

"Put me through," I said calmly, but my uneasiness was escalating. Regardless of my experience and the numerous successful transactions I have completed, I couldn't suppress a shiver of anticipation that always accompanied my work.

"Good afternoon, Mr. Gerald. How are you today?"

I was expecting this call all morning.

"Hi Mr. Harvey. I'm doing well and you? "

"I'm just fine. Thanks for asking."

"I hope things have developed positively for us and that your client is ready to sign the contract."

"I'm sorry to disappoint you, Mr. Gerald, but my client received a better offer and...."

"How is it possible?"

I could not hide my amazement. "Someone made a better offer?"

"Your offer was the best until the last moment when a more attractive offer was made and my client took it."

"Yes, I understand. Thank you for your call."

"I need to thank you for your understanding. I hope that we will work together again soon."

I hung up feeling I was in a dream and nothing I heard was true. However, the handset was still in my hand. The conversation did happen.

The loss of this deal was a serious blow to my credibility and confidence. The worst part was it was the second consecutive potential deal that had fallen through at the last minute. Surely, if the board voted to participate in the new energy project, it would be my last chance to redeem myself.

There is a lot of competition. There are many young aggressive and ruthless people in the industry. People who are using their computer skills and the Internet to make as much money in days as our parents made in decades. One of these predators had stolen this deal from under my nose. He'd found out the details of our offer and waited until the last minute to present a better offer ensuring that I would not have an opportunity to renegotiate.

But how could they know? There was something wrong here. Who was giving confidential information to a competitor?

* * *

I got up, went to the office bar and poured a large glass of scotch. I thought nothing can stop me from taking a big shot of scotch, but suddenly I remembered that Elliott should be notified about the latest events. He absolutely forbade drinking alcohol during working hours, so I put my glass down and went to his office.

I was sitting in his office waiting for his reaction to my conversation with Harvey, and expecting him to be angry with me.

"It is definitely bad news, but the odds may not be always on our side," Elliott told me after I explained what had happened.

"You have to get used to the idea that in this business, sometimes it's possible to lose a potential customer."

I stared at him incredulously.

What happened to this man? He was speaking calmly trying to reassure me that it was okay. His normal reaction in such situations would have been to dump all the celestial lightning on my head.

"Next time you will be more successful."

"Sure."

"Tell me, what's wrong? Why do you look so distressed? Or are you just tired and stressed as VP?"

"Nothing like that. I'm just disappointed with the results. After all the hard work."

"If there is something more don't hesitate to tell me."

"Okay."

He got up, went closer to me and said:

"I have to ask."

"Okay?"

"I need a person I really trust to visit our office and our branches in Toronto. It will take probably a month, two max. What do you think?"

"It will be a kind of auditing or...."

"Yes, it's auditing, but I want you to treat it like it is just routine visit. I usually go myself, to see how things are going and to present our new services and future goals. In addition, I announce any new programs and awards for the employees."

"Sounds interesting. When do you want me to go?"

"What about next week?"

"Okay."

"Perfect. I'll meet you on Monday and give you the particulars and specific directions. You can prepare a PowerPoint presentation or you can organize and facilitate workshops. How you communicate the information is up to you. In addition, I'll give you a list of clients I want you to meet. You will be busy, son. No time for drinking and fun. I will email the manager of the Toronto office to tell him that my nephew will be coming to represent me at the annual meeting."

Now, I realize why Elliott was so suspiciously friendly and cooperative. He would do anything to keep me far away from Lucy. I wish I had shouted into his face: "Do you think I'm so stupid?"

"Thank you for the opportunity, Elliott," I said instead.

"You are welcome. I truly believe it will be a great experience for you as a future Senior Vice President."

Bastard!

CHAPTER FOUR

It was a sunny spring afternoon when my plane landed at Pearson airport. The company car was waiting for me and the driver was holding the door open for me.

"Good afternoon, sir. Welcome to Toronto," he said with respect.

"Good afternoon. You have wonderful weather here."

"Oh, yeah. The spring is lovely this year."

I have been to Toronto a couple of times and I always admired the beautiful blue sky of this city. Today the sky was really beautiful, clear and a deep blue.

* * *

I remembered the latest instructions and stats Elliott had given me before I left. "Canada has avoided many of the problems that affected the U.S., such as the huge public debt crisis in the banking system, the housing "bubble" and a weakened currency. Also the Canadian banking system remained stable during the global credit crisis and was characterized as the strongest in the world. Despite debt crises in Europe affecting countries such as Greece, Spain, and Italy as a result of rising sovereign debt levels, Canada's banks continued to perform well and remain stable. Even the U.S. President admitted that in a speech: "Canada has shown us that it is a very good manager of the financial system. We considered Canada as one of the safest countries where to invest."

The head office of our company was on Bay Street in the financial district. The traffic in downtown Toronto was congested and the driver was showing very strong driving skills enabling him to navigate and move forward quickly. The city was different from the last time I had been here two years ago. The high-rise condominium construction business was booming and many of the old houses had just disappeared. Our bank and family business have invested in the Toronto real estate market and we now invested in condo buildings close to Lake Ontario.

* * *

In the end of June, Elliott called me at the office.

"Hey Robert. How's everything?"

"Everything's good. How are you?"

"I am doing pretty well, thanks. I actually want to tell you that I'm very satisfied with your work in Toronto. I liked your idea about the new design of the branches, the new colours and stuff. Also, I liked the idea of opening bank cafes and offering self-serving coffee to the clients in our branches."

"Thanks, sir."

"I can see you are capable of creative thinking when you have a chance to work independently. I was thinking of giving you this chance. Would you be interested in overseeing the family business in Canada; it will be a promotion. The next step will be a senior vice president. It's an amazing career path don't you think?"

"You are doing all this to keep me far from Lucy, aren't you?"

"There has nothing to do with Lucy. I think she knows what she needs to do. She just graduated. In the fall she is going to Harvard."

"She doesn't want to go to Harvard."

"She will do what has to be done as there are no other options. Let's do our job. I want you to rent another floor in the building to accommodate your own permanent office, hire additional staff at your discretion. When you are settled, I want you to see how we can expand into other provinces in Canada. We have had pretty good results in Quebec, BC and Nova Scotia so far, but we need to expand."

* * *

Elliott was right when he said I would be very busy and would not have any spare time for fun. The only thing I could find time to do outside of my duties in the bank was to go to the gym. There is a Goodlife Fitness gym in the underground mall in my office complex so I could work out regularly. There is a bright side to work. Summers in Toronto are very hot and humid and it is better to stay in air-conditioned rooms and avoid going outside too much.

This is how I spent my summer. No vacation, no fun. I missed Lucy very much despite the fact that we talked every day by Skype.

One day in the beginning of September Lucy called me on my cell.

"Are you still staying at the Hilton?"

"No, why?"

"Because I need to tell the taxi driver where to go."

"Where are you?"

"Ha, ha, at Pearson."

"You are in Toronto? Seriously? Why didn't you tell me you were coming?"

"It's a surprise."

"It really is."

"I hope it is a nice surprise."

"More than pleasant. Okay we'll talk later. I'm at the King George Hotel. The Royal suite. I will wait for you there."

"Where are you now? In the office?"

"Yes, I'm at work but it's not too far from the hotel. Anyway, it will take you some time to drive from Pearson to the hotel. It will be rush hour very soon."

"All right, Bob. See you there."

"Perfect. See you soon."

"Can't wait."

"Me too."

I told my secretary that I was leaving for the day and rushed to the hotel to make sure everything there was okay. The hotel's staff did their job perfectly. The room was clean, the bed sheets had been changed and the air conditioner was spreading the fresh smell of pine. After more than an hour the receptionist called me to say I had visitor. "Let her in," I said and felt happy that I would see Lucy in a few minutes.

"Bobby, I missed you so much."

"I missed you too, kiddo." I said when she jumped on me and

hugged me. I kissed her on the mouth. The kiss wasn't one shared by relatives. She looked at me, scared. She pushed me back.

"What are you doing here?" I asked to hide my confusion.

"I accepted the offer of admission of Ryerson University."

"Ryerson? What program?"

"Not finance for sure. I enrolled in the fashion design program."

"Unbelievable. Does your Daddy know that you are here?"

She laughed sounding like a bad kid.

"Of course he doesn't."

"So, what are we doing now?"

I knew we were in trouble.

"We are going to face the biggest fear - The Beast."

Before she could finish the sentence, my cell rang.

"Robert, where are you?"

"The Beast." I covered the phone and told Lucy.

"I'm at the hotel right now."

"Is Lucy with you?"

"Yes, she's here."

"I'm in Toronto. My plane just landed at Pearson. I want to talk to both of you immediately. Can I have the address of the hotel, please?"

"Sure."

For the second time today, I gave the address.

"Is he already here?" asked Lucy when I ended the call.

"Yeah, he is on his way."

"The Beast is very fast, isn't he?"

"He took the flight right after you did. But you said that you didn't tell him."

"I called mom. From the airport. I didn't want to scare them, but I didn't want them to stop me."

"I see. Your mom told him."

"I was expecting him to come after me."

"Oh yeah?"

"Really. But I didn't expect him to show up on the same day."

"Are you scared?"

"A little bit. But I'm ready to stand up for my right to be independent. And you, are you scared of him?"

"I'm scared of him, but I am determined to fight for our right to make our own decisions about our personal life."

"That's amazing, Bobby!"

"Before Elliott comes, I want to tell you something very important. I was avoiding telling you, but it is time to tell you the truth."

* * *

"She's with you, right?" said Elliott when I opened the door.

"Yes. She's here. Come in," I said, feeling shivers going down my spine as they usually do when around him.

He entered and looked around to try to find her.

She appeared from the kitchen.

He rushed to hug her.

"Lucy, my dear. You're driving us crazy, how could you do this to us? Lucy, you know we love you. Please, baby, please forgive us and come back home."

"Oh, Daddy...."

She ran to him and nestled in his arms.

"Sorry Dad, I didn't want to scare you. I love you too."

"Honey, I'm here for you. Just say what you want and I'll do it for you right away. I promise."

"Dad, I would like to take the design management program at Ryerson."

Elliott was still keeping her in his hands, scared that she'll run away from him again.

"Whatever you want, dear. I will finish with some transactions in the office and I'll come to help you here."

"That is not what I meant. I want to do everything myself."

"Don't be ridiculous, honey. You'll need help. I will buy you a condo close to the university."

Elliott wasn't ready to let her fly away from the nest. He wasn't ready at all. For him she was still his little baby. Lucy's eyes were full of tears when she said:

"Robert's here, Dad. We plan to live together."

Elliott turned to me and said, eyes filled with horror:

"Don't tell me that you already...."

I had been watching the whole scene silently only now deciding to speak up. Nervously, I said:

"No, we didn't, but we like each other."

He looked at Lucy. She nodded.

"It is absolutely unacceptable. You are very close relatives and it is not going to work." His voice was harsh and cold as ice.

"Elliott, can I talk to you in private about that issue?"

"There is nothing to talk about."

Lucy hugged him again but remained silent.

My throat was dry. I swallowed painfully and mustered up enough courage to say:

"Trust me, there is. Lucy, I'm sorry can you please go to my bedroom, so I can talk to Elliott for a moment. Have something to drink if you want. We won't be long."

Lucy left. Elliott was still standing in the middle of the room.

"Have a seat, Elliott. I'm about to tell you something very important and it's best if you're sitting."

His face was tense as he sat on the sofa. I sat on the chair next to him. A difficult conversation was ahead.

"How could you do this? You're cousins!" he said nervously, as if expecting to hear something terrible.

I kept silent for a moment, trying to find the right words. Slowly, I began to speak.

"I have not forgotten that fact, but I don't have a blood connection with her as my father was adopted. I was always accepted as one of the family but we're not relatives, so I cannot see any problem."

There was a long pause. He was looking at me in disbelief. Finally, he spoke:

"No way."

" I know it's shocking news for you but this is the truth. My Dad, your brother Ted, was adopted."

I could see how his face was changing its colors from white to red and to white again while he was processing my words.

"How do you know he was adopted? Who told you?"

"My father."

"He knew about that as well? How? I don't understand. I can't believe this. Who told him?"

"Grandfather Robert himself."

Elliott was perfectly trained to hide his emotions and to keep a poker face in any stressful situation, but right now his facade wasn't working. I could feel the pain in his voice when he said:

"How long have you known?"

"My father told me just before he died."

Elliott looked at me, fear evident in his eyes as he knew this was only the beginning of the bad news.

"Do you know why he decided to reveal the secret exactly at that time?"

"He said that something bad might happen to him and he wanted me to know the truth."

Elliott's face was as white as a bone. He looked scared.

"He said that? He said something bad might happen to him? Did he say more about it?"

"Nope."

"Why haven't you told me sooner about this?"

"My father asked me not to. He wasn't sure if there was any real danger or if it was only his imagination."

"I don't know what to say. I'm speechless for the first time in my life."

"I felt the same way when he told me."

"I still don't understand why your father was adopted before all the other kids were born."

"My father was the son of my grandfather's high school sweetheart. They were planning to get married after graduation. However, Daniel Gerald had already arranged a marriage for his son. Daniel's father had arranged a financially advantageous marriage for him. It was a good move for the family and Daniel wanted to do the same thing with his children. He persuaded grandfather to agree to the arranged marriage because it was good for the family, but grandfather never forgot his first love. A couple of years later, before she died of injuries sustained in a car crash, she asked him to take care of her son as her husband was dead. Grandfather took the boy, who was six month old at that time, and went to work at the London office. When the family returned it consisted of two sons - my father and Uncle Oliver. I don't know why Grandfather insisted on keeping it a secret."

Elliott was thinking about something.

I continued.

"Now you understand why not give it to Ted, right?"

He looked at me with an expression in his face saying, "How are you reading my thoughts?"

We stayed silent for a moment and then he said slowly:

"My father loved Ted very much; even more than the others. I didn't understand why I got the Presidency. Now everything is clear."

"My father thought everything grandfather did was fair. He said it is very important for me to know the truth and that's why he was breaking his promise to keep the secret."

"I cannot imagine that someone wanted to kill him."

"Me neither."

"I need to do something about it. If he told you, he could be in danger then that changes everything. We need to be sure what exactly happened."

"I did some research but didn't find anything other than what officials told us."

"I will take care of it now. Damn it! I guess you told Lucy already."

I nodded.

"The first part only. I didn't want to tell her that my father might have been killed."

"You did the right thing. I know she loves you."

"I hope so. I love her too."

"Do you have some scotch around? I really need a strong drink."

"I have some here. I can call room service. Do you want to order dinner or go to the hotel's restaurant?"

"Just give me a sip of what you have here. I need to go back to New York tonight. I have a very important meeting in the morning. The investment deals for Greece and Spain. We need to finalize the negotiations tomorrow."

"I will tell Lucy to join us. Here is the bottle. I will bring glasses from the kitchen."

Lucy and I returned to the living room with the glasses. I poured scotch for the three of us while Lucy took a cigarette from her purse and lit it with a small gold lighter encrusted with diamonds. I had never seen her smoking in the presence of Elliott.

Elliott didn't say anything.

* * *

The whisky bottle was gone in the blink of an eye as all of us needed a big shot. Elliott slowly calmed down, but his thoughts were clearly somewhere else. At least now he was able to suppress and hide his real feelings and fears. It's not difficult for him. He is a professional player. But it was too much to handle right now. It was too much stress, even for him.

"Well, Lucy, I'll go back to New York. You take care of your-selves here. I hope you will enjoy your studies and later we will see. Once you have a degree you can take your Master's at Harvard. You could enroll in the design program there."

"Okay, Daddy. I'll think about it. Maybe I'll change my mind and enroll at New York University. I don't mind the idea of Harvard, but its program is not exactly what I want."

"Alright dear. I assume you were shocked to learn that Robert is not a blood relation."

"Yeah, but deep in my heart I already knew that. He's so dif-ferent from all of us. Not only in his appearance. He's the only one with black hair and black eyes. He is different from all of us in his behaviour; I mean he is more spiritual, and not so obsessed with money like all Geralds. I could say the same about Uncle Ted. It was kind of obvious they are not typical Geralds. I never thought he was adopted, but I knew he was different."

Elliott turned his whole body towards her. His eyes were wide open in surprise. He hugged Lucy and said:

"I'm impressed with your observational skills, Lucy. I have to confess I never thought about all that."

" I told you Dad, don't underestimate me."

Elliot was looking at her with a strange expression. It was dif-ficult for him to accept the fact that his small baby girl has turned to an independent young woman.

"I won't my love, I won't."

He took his glass and drank the content in one single sip. The colour started to return on his face. From my own experience I knew that drinking might help you forget why you want to drink but it's not going to resolve any of your problems. I asked him:

"How do you feel, Elliott? Sorry I put you through all this."

"It's not your fault. I've been such a fool all these years."

"Do you want me to drive you to the airport, Elliott?"

"That might be necessary, I don't feel that great. Thanks."

CHAPTER FIVE

Later in bed, Lucy told me:

"I knew it. I knew that you are different from the rest of the Geralds. That's why I fell in love with you."

"I love you too sweetheart. In the beginning, I just liked you very much but I fell in love with you when I started knowing you better."

"I'm crazy about you!"

"So you were ready to have sex with me even if I was your cousin?"

"Yeah. From the time I saw you at Eddy's party."

"And you were ready to confront everyone, even Elliott."

"I already did when I came here to live with you. I can take this program in NY."

"You were ready to lose all your money and your family as well?"

She laughed.

"I could care less about all that. I knew you would never dare to oppose my father, so I did it for both of us."

"Are you sure you are not adopted too?"

"I'm a true Gerald."

"I still love you," I kissed her and then we made love forgetting about all the similarities and differences that existed in the Gerald family.

The next morning we made love again and she asked:

"Do you still love your ex-wife? Dad told me you were crazy about her and started drinking a lot after she left you."

"Are you jealous? After ten years?"

"Should I be? After ten years?"

"Then you need to know that there is no reason to be jealous."

* * *

My ex-wife Nora was an ordinary club singer who became a lady,

49

as in the Cinderella story. She was my first love.

Even now I can remember clearly the first day I met her.

It was my nineteenth birthday and me, a group of friends and Eddy, at that time we were inseparable. We decided to go to an elite club. We knew that the club we chose had a good band and would serve us alcohol. They would serve tequila even to an infant.

Nora was one of the performers that evening, and when she came on stage my breath stopped. She was fantastic - small but nicely rounded where necessary. She had the most beautiful blond hair which fell to her shoulders in light waves. Her eyes were huge with a wonderful, attractive sparkle. She wore a skin-tight mini-dress, which provided a view of her slender and shapely legs and showed off her small waist. Its deep neckline revealed the finest, sexiest bust I have ever seen. I felt as if I had been hit by a lightning bolt and I couldn't catch my breath. I knew it was love at first sight.

"Are you deaf?" asked Eddy. "Three times I have asked you if you want some marijuana and you didn't hear me."

"Excuse me. I don't want any. In fact, give me a little."

"So, what you are staring at, man?"

"The singer, stupid. See the singer?"

"What?"

"Look at the babe who's singing? Isn't she gorgeous?"

"The singer? Well, not too bad."

"She's just incredibly sexy."

"I don't believe it will be a problem, to have her."

"Will you come with me behind the stage to try?"

"Sure."

We continued to dance with our dates until Nora finished the last song. By then we were high on alcohol and drugs which made us bold and aggressive. We left our friends and went with uncertain steps behind the stage to look for Nora Santana.

We were stopped by a huge bodyguard.

"Guys, where do you think you are going?" he said with a strong Spanish accent.

"We want to get an autograph from Miss Santana," I said confidently.

"She is not giving any here. Please leave the hall."

"But we...."

"Come on," we got unceremoniously manhandled and without any effort he threw us out of the club.

The fresh air cleared our dizzy heads, but it didn't reduce my desire to meet my beloved, so we stood at the door, waiting for Nora.

It took nearly an hour before she appeared, followed by the bodyguard.

She was wearing jeans and a sweater, but she seemed even sexier.

"Miss Santana," I said politely. "Let me pay my tribute."

"Who are these fools?" she asked the bodyguard.

"Again, you two," said the gorilla, who was about to remove us out of the way.

"Just a second," I said despite the risk that he might break my arm. "Would you give me your address or phone...."

"What insolence!" the guard said.

"Come, Fernando. Hurry!" said Nora.

"I would like to invite you to have dinner," I cried the moment that bodyguard swung and Eddy and his glasses flew to the pavement. At that time he was still wearing glasses which he thought was cool because he was obsessed with Harry Potter. When he became a movie star he changed his mind and now wears contact lenses.

"Fernando, get them out of my way," she said and the order was executed immediately. I found myself lying next to Eddie's s glasses on the pavement before Nora got into a huge Cadillac and I called out:

"Perhaps you think I'm a crazy fan, but that is not true. I have strong and sincere feelings, and the most serious intentions towards you."

Nobody answered me and the car slowly drove away.

"The best would be if you both go home and sober up," said one of the club's bouncers, who had heard shouting and had came to see what was happening.

Neither of us answered him.

"Come on, go away from here," he said again and smashed Eddy's glasses totally.

"Damn," Eddy said. "I cannot see anything. Where are my glasses?"

"I'm afraid that after the bodyguard stepped on what was left of them, you cannot use them anymore. Come, let's get a cab."

The next day we went back to the club. But she paid absolutely no attention to me. Each night for two weeks we went to the club and each

night her bodyguard waited for us in front of her dressing room. The drill
was the same. He was just throwing us out on the street.

One evening, she came to our table.

"You said you want to invite me to have dinner. I will accept your
invitation, but I'm free tomorrow only."

"Then, see you tomorrow," I said huskily, and could not believe my
ears. I didn't understand what caused this change in her attitude, but I
was so deep in love that I didn't suspect anything dishonorable. Like a
fool I thought she had fallen for me.

I didn't know that her lover the bodyguard had checked me out. The
bastard! After he found out that I was one of the richest heirs in America,
he had told her to marry me, so they could have a great future, paid for
with my money. I can imagine what he told her: "This is a golden bird
perched on your shoulder. Look how young and naive he is. Furthermore,
he has swallowed the hook completely. He is here every night. It won't be
a problem for you to take him to the altar. And then we will live as kings
and queens."

* * *

The next day we went to dinner and our affair started. I had dated
a number of girls before I met Nora and was no virgin. But after that first
night with Nora, I realized that compared to her, I was an innocent angel.
She had more sexual experience, was sensual and passionate and not
restrained in bed. I thought that maybe she could make even a dead man
make love with her. She had an enormous and tight bust, the best I'd ever
touched. We made love until morning, and when she left me in the bed, I
felt I had been squeezed like a lemon. I realized that this was my first real
love affair.

I was so crazy about her that I postponed my studies at Harvard for
one year so that we could be together. We had been dating for two months
when I asked her to become my wife.

"I'm so incredibly happy." she chirped.

"Does that mean yes?"

"Oh, yeah I do."

"Let's celebrate it. I'll call Eddy."

"Honey, are you sure you want me to stop working?" she asked me
a few days later.

"It doesn't matter to me. If you enjoy singing, I do not mind if you continue to do so."

"I would the like role of Mrs. Gerald more."

"There is no need to play the role of Mrs. Gerald, my dear. You will be Mrs. Gerald."

But it wasn't so easy and achievable, because my whole family stood against our marriage.

Everyone, except Grandfather Robert.

* * *

Grandfather Robert was *the only one who stood by my side and gave me a hand. One day he called and asked me to go and see him at the Big House.*

We call our family mansion in East New York the Big House. It was purchased by Daniel Gerald, our great-grandfather and it was where Grandfather Robert and Grandmother Margaret lived and raised their five children: Ted, Ben, Oliver, Melanie and Elliott. The children left, married and had families of their own. All of them have summer homes. However, the grandchildren spend their summers at the Big House. It was where we spent our childhoods. It is a nice memory.

Grandfather Robert was big and good looking man. Silver threads in his temples made him look very distinguished and regal.

"Come in, Robert," he said with a slightly raspy voice.

We sat down in his familiar and large living room and he began:

"Your father asked me to exert my influence on you to change your mind about this marriage. A martini?"

"Yes. What are you going to do now? Give me one of you sermons?"

"No. I'll give you some advice. Fight for your love, Robert. When I was your age I loved a girl. The family opposed the marriage as it does now."

"What happened?"

"I wasn't strong enough and finally the family won. Your great-grandfather Daniel was a cruel man. I allowed my father to persuade me to marry Margaret Anne Tarningam."

"I thought you and grandmother have a happy marriage"

"We are happy. We are friends. We feel respect and affection for each other, but not love. Notwithstanding the absence of these feelings,

Margaret is an excellent wife and mother. She really is a wonderful, unique woman."

"I've heard that very often, love comes after marriage. Maybe you have not noticed."

"Our marriage was a business deal. It resulted in the merger of our fathers' money, but we did not go into the marriage with our hearts. I could not love her as I loved Maggie, my first love. I think she tried to love me, but failed. Both of us left our hearts in our youth, and souls along with our first loves."

"How could you live in a loveless marriage for so many years?"

"It has been awful, trust me. You have to fight for this woman. Don't give up. Remember that I'll be there for you."

He didn't tell me that I actually was the grandson of his Maggie.

I stood up to the family, but it wasn't easy.

"I don't want to hear a word about a wedding," said my mom with anger. "Forget it. Go back to Harvard?! Don't you know your relationship with this girl is damaging your future? I can't believe that I raised such a selfish man, Robert Gerald."

"I don't intend to listen to you."

"What do you want, to become a loser? So far, there has never been a stripper in our family."

"Nora is not a stripper."

"Well, she is a woman with a bad reputation. I know how and what has turned your head. You are naive. Don't you know that she is after your money?"

"What you are saying is so awful."

We got married secretly by an accommodating priest and tried to put an end to the objections.

When I told my mother about the marriage she said, "That woman will not set a foot in my house," and I was afraid my wife and I would find ourselves homeless.

When I told Grandfather Robert, he said "You are brave and deserve to be happy," and he gave us an apartment in one of the bank-owned buildings to live in.

* * *

Two months later Nora told me she was pregnant and I went mad with joy.

Grandfather Robert made me a proposition. If I returned to and completed my studies at Harvard I would be given a job at the bank as a
trainee in the Financial Analysis department. I accepted at once because
my money was running out and I needed to support my family.

One day I came home from work early and decided to surprise Nora.
I didn't ring the door bell and carefully unlocked the door with my key
and quietly walked to the bedroom. I heard voices inside the bedroom. One
was Nora's and the other was a man's whose voice I did not recognize,
but it seemed familiar. But who was it?

"I cannot wait. I need money."

"Please, Fernando. I have no money."

"You don't have money? Why then did you marry this rich roos-
ter?"

"I'm telling you I don't have money now."

"I don't care. When we planned for you to marry this rich guy you
told me:

"I'll give you a lot of money. I'll make your life amazing" And what
happened? So far you gave me a few small handouts."

"I told you that his family did not want us to marry."

"Don't talk fables. You're a Gerald, one of the richest families in
America."

"But I have no money, don't you understand? Why did you come
here now? To ruin everything?"

"Listen to me now, doll. You aren't the one that will dictate the
terms. What did you think? That when you become a lady I would disappear? Actually, you're a bitch."

"Stop it."

"No. No. I'm not going to stop. We've got a deal."

"Okay. Robert gave me some family jewelry. I will sell them and give
you all the money. Maybe then you will decide to go away somewhere."

"Maybe yes, maybe no. But hurry because if you don't, I will come
back here and tell your rich bastard about our deal and our hot games in
the motel. I'll tell him also that you had an abortion so you could marry
him. You were three months pregnant with my child. You killed my son
to become a rich lady and I want to be compensated for the loss."

"You convinced me to do it."

"It didn't take much effort to convince you. It was very easy for you *to leave me and to kill our child. You sold us for money. That is a fact."*

"Get out!"

"No tricks, baby. You are not an innocent virgin. How long has it been since we did it, eh?"

"Stay away from me. Don't you dare touch me."

He grabbed her and started kissing her.

"Enough!" I cried as I walked into the room. They looked at me horrified. "Get out of my house. Both of you!"

"Oh, Robert, dear, let me explain."

"Everything is clear. You cheated on me".

"Please listen to me. I really love you and I've been faithful since I married you."

"Do you expect me to believe you?"

"It is the truth. I married for money, but then I fell in love with you."

"Get out. I don't want to see you again."

"Robert, don't say that, I am begging you. Remember I'm carrying your child. You cannot just throw me out."

"It is not my child."

"Sir! Please, listen," said the man and pissed me off totally.

"If both of you don't leave my apartment immediately, I will call the police."

They went.

Nora was sobbing, her lover trying in vain to calm her.

I filed immediately for divorce.

* * *

"I warned you," said my mother.

"You don't deserve this," my grandfather said.

"Let's get drunk," was John's and Eddie's response to the news, and so we went and got drunk.

With the help of the family lawyer, Nora was persuaded to leave town. I was relieved because it seemed impossible for me to breathe the same air as she did.

It was a gloomy autumn day when she called me and said we have a son. I knew he wasn't mine. The test confirmed that I am not the child's father. That was the moment I started drinking.

CHAPTER SIX

Lucy and I lived in the hotel for a month before deciding to move into a condominium. Once we decided to move I arranged to meet with a real estate agent the next day at the Balzac Cafe in the Distillery District. We ate breakfast at the hotel and decided to walk to the caf? so I could show Lucy this part of the city. We had enough time. The meeting was at 2 p.m.

* * *

We were walking along King Street and admiring an old church when we saw a group of people in the park next to the church. They were protestors, carrying different posters.

"Is that Occupy Toronto? I didn't know they were still protesting," said Lucy.

"Oh no, it should be something else. I have seen them here in this park a couple of times, but it was a long time ago when I visited Toronto with my Dad."

"They haven't achieved any success so far, have they?"

I looked at her, I was surprised by her comment and took a few moments before I answered.

"Not really. Actually, the movement started here in Canada. In Vancouver. "

"I know. It was a magazine or something. I kind of empathize with the movement, but my father was furious."

I smiled remembering how angry Elliott was about them.

"Yeah. He was. I remember when they blocked Wall Street in September. Some of them were yelling in front of our office that bankers are a threat to the global economy, they are like sharks, that banking and financial speculation is a form of financial terrorism."

Lucy walked for a moment not speaking and then said:

"I think that money should be distributed more fairly in the world. Don't you think so?"

It was my turn to walk in silence for a while. Finally, I said.

"I do, but unfortunately that is not going to happen."

"It is a pity. I hate money. Honestly."

Her face was so serious. She was so naive and innocent. I didn't know what to tell her. I started with hesitation:

"Well, I really don't have much time to reflect on that, but if you don't have money you couldn't do any of the things you love to do. Money is an important part of every society, whether we like it or not."

"True, but I don't want to work in finance; I don't want to be a banker. I want to set up my own business, doing work that is meaningful to me."

"You will need money to start a business and the start up cost of a small business is initially very high."

"I understand that. I feel so confused. I was thinking about a business model where I could share my profit with someone in need. For example, I design a dress, set the price at twice the cost to make and distribute the dress. I would give the profits of every second dress sold and keep the rest of the profits."

"It sounds very interesting. We can fine-tune that model together."

* * *

We reached Balzac at 1:30. It is a two storey Grand Parisian style cafe, very charming and cosy. Chandeliers, posters and tile floor give off a comforting vibe. I fell in love with these types of cafes and espresso coffee bars during my visit to Paris last year. Paris cafes are the meeting place, the rendez-vous spot, and a networking source, and a place to relax or to refuel. Lucy liked Balzac very much and I promised to take her to Paris next summer.

We ordered a Cafe Latte and a double cappuccino with a vanilla-ricotta croissant and vanilla-almond biscotti. We were enjoying the food when the realtor showed up. She didn't want to drink espresso, so I ordered regular North American coffee for her. We had a short conversation, explained what were looking for and she told us about a number of available condos for rent. Three of them sounded like they might be good options for us. We asked to see them right way. She gave a short tour of the condos, which were located in the west end of downtown Toronto. We chose one of the condos as soon as we saw it.

It was on the top floor of one of the most modern buildings in the city. It offered many amenities and luxuries including electronic gates, a security guard, maid service, and valet service. It was a skyscraper built using the latest technology, made of steel and glass. Its glass towers had a large private rooftop space for the tenants and there were beautiful gardens on balconies.

Its marble foyer was opulent and beautifully landscaped with a variety of rare plant species that any botanical garden would envy. In keeping with the opulence of the building, staff - concierge, security and elevator operators and maintenance workers all wore elegant, expensive uniforms. It was difficult to impress us. We are used to luxury and splendor, but we could not deny that this is one posh and cool place.

The apartment was really great. It was arranged by the skilled hands of a professional. The furniture, simple and unpretentious, was functional, ergonomic and obviously expensive. The view of Lake Ontario was breathtaking and that "million dollar view" actually sold us on this condo.

We settled into this, our love nest, very nicely. We hoped that we could stay here a couple of years. I thought that maybe Elliott did me a favor by sending me to come to Toronto. I can work independently here and Lucy can study. We can be free here, far from the family's control.

* * *

September. October and November went very pleasantly. Lucy enjoyed her studies and worked on some interesting design projects. We also traveled a lot across Canada as a part of my mission to visit our branches in all provinces. We visited Ottawa, Quebec City, Montreal, Vancouver, Calgary, and Halifax.

In the middle of December, we went back to New York for the Christmas holidays. It is a tradition in our family to get together at the Big House during the holidays.

After the Christmas dinner, Elliott asked me to come back to

New York.

"Robert, I instigated a private investigation and the detective found some suspicious things, related to Ben's and your father's death. Lately some other suspicious incidents have happened at the bank. I think someone is playing some dirty games against us. This is not the place or the time to talk but the situation is serious. I need you here. Try to convince Lucy to attend New York University."

"Okay, Uncle."

PART TWO

PAMELA

CHAPTER ONE

"**L**ucy is in Toronto." I yelled to Elliott over the phone.

"What is she doing in Toronto for God's sake?" Elliott gasped.

"She just called me from Pearson airport and said she has accepted a letter of admission to Ryerson University."

"What?"

"Ryerson University. She will be taking a Fashion Design program."

"Are you telling me she will be studying in Toronto instead of Harvard?"

"She just told me."

There was silence. I knew he was angry.

"It is entirely your fault," he said finally.

"Excuse me?"

"How did you allow this to happen?"

"It's not my fault. It is yours. You have always allowed her to do whatever she wants."

"Is she okay? Oh my God! Is she okay?"

"She's fine. She sounded very excited."

"Was she alone?"

"I think so. I don't know actually. Why?"

"I'm going to Toronto. I'll call the pilot to prepare the plane."

"I'll come with you."

"You better stay here. I'll take care of it. Anyway, you did enough."

He hung up.

Oh, yes. I am responsible for everything that goes wrong in this family.

* * *

I married Elliott when I was nineteen.
He was thirty two.
He was the first and only man in my life.

My father, the reputable and very rich investment banker Kevin Fletcher, was determined to give me a good education, and I was all set to go and study in London in the fall. But in April I met Elliott at a party my father organized every year to raise money for charity.

I fell crazy in love, but was too scared to tell my Dad that I would not leave New York for anything in the world. Elliott realized I wasn't able to confront my family and made an official proposal to my father. Elliott Gerald was a good candidate for marriage and it was a "yes" from my Dad.

We got married in October. Elliott was pushing me to enroll in New York University, but I was not ambitious and chose to focus on my role as Mrs. Elliott Gerald.

* * *

After the wedding and our amazing honeymoon in Europe we had a wonderful time together. It was an endless round of parties, gala dinners, balls, operas, theatre. Every weekend we were at the most prestigious restaurants, then dancing until midnight in chic clubs.

We were at the famous club "Friends" to see their new Saturday night show when I suddenly threw up and felt I might faint.

"I'm dying," I told Elliott.

He was so scared and didn't know what to do.

He called an ambulance. In the hospital they performed tests and during the ultrasound the doctor told us I was pregnant - five weeks. He showed us a small dark spot on the screen. We couldn't believe that the small thing in the middle was our future baby.

"Congratulations!" the doctor said, and gave us an ultrasound picture as proof that a new life was growing inside of me.

We were so happy, so excited.

After that evening, I had no more symptoms, and my pregnancy was going very well.

I felt perfect.

Two months before my due date, tragedy happened.

I was going to my doctor when a cab hit our car at a busy intersection. My driver was killed on impact. It was a miracle that I was sitting in the back seat and on the other side of the car. Otherwise I wouldn't have survived.

The last thing I remember was the car approaching. I couldn't do anything, not even move. Then the world fell into darkness.

* * *

When I woke up *the first thing I saw was Elliott's worried face. He told me that we had a daughter and everything would be okay.*

I didn't remember what happened.

After a couple days the whole horror came back into my memory. I spent over a month in the hospital.

I was in hell.

The flashbacks were driving me crazy. I felt like the crash was happening again. Every night I had the same nightmares - a car was coming towards me and I was paralysed, not able to escape from being hit.

After I left the hospital, it took me a long time to overcome the trauma and return to normal. That's the reason I stated seeing my first psychotherapist, Doctor Milligan.

When my medical doctors thought that I was strong enough to hear and survive terrible news my family doctor explained that after the accident I required life-saving surgery and because of the extent of my injuries I could not have more children. I fell back into a deep depression. I didn't allow Elliott to even touch me and wasn't able to enjoy the child I already had.

At the same time Elliott became manic that he would lose his daughter and became an overprotective parent. As time passed he became more and more obsessed with our little girl and would do anything for her.

She was everything to him.

She was a Daddy's girl.

I loved our Lucy. Elliott worshipped her. In my opinion we had to be good parents, but not overprotective parents.

* * *

When Lucy *was sixteen she experienced her "first love" disappointment. With feminine intuition I understood the reason for the changes in her behavior, while Elliott didn't even realize that his daughter was suffering over a boy.*

She became depressed. I knew the symptoms.

I wanted to establish a closer relationship with her, and offered to talk to her woman to woman, but she refused.

Then she began to eat. A lot. It was like she wanted to swallow up everything that she saw.

One day I saw her vomiting in her bathroom and when I asked what was going on she just slammed the door. While she was at school I checked her room. I was so shocked when I found bottles of laxatives hidden inside the toilet cabinet.

"Lucy, what are you doing, for God's sake? You'll kill yourself like that," I told her. "Let me help you. Please."

"Leave me alone," she answered me contemptuously. "I can handle it myself."

"I was in a similar situation after the accident."

She interrupted me rudely.

"Can you stop right now? I have heard that story a hundred times."

* * *

"You should consult with a specialist in eating disorders," Elliott told me." We cannot leave it like that. She wants to kill herself. Look at her! She is a walking skeleton. You need to call our family doctor for a referral right away. Go to Google and research more about anorexia, bulimia and stuff. I'll Google it too. Book an appointment and I'll talk to you in the evening."*

I arranged an appointment with a specialist and somehow convinced Lucy to go there. Elliott was scared to death. He refused to come with us.

* * *

Lucy slumped down in a chair in the waiting room. She was staring blankly at the wall not saying a word.*

I walked in alone to explain what was going on.

"Let me talk to her in private. I need to do an initial assessment. Then I can give you a proper diagnosis," the doctor told me.

It was my turn to stare at the wall in the waiting room.

What to do?

She could die!

I needed Elliott; I needed him there, right then.

66

But he wasn't there.

* * *

When she came out *of the doctor's office, the doctor asked to speak to me in private.*

"Lucy gave me permission to share our conversation. Unfortunately you're right. A typical case of a patient who resists, I'm afraid that at this stage, Mrs. Gerald, she's not at all motivated to heal."

"What will we do then?"

"We'll try to change things. Please, convince her to start sessions with me. With an integrated approach of medication, psychotherapy, and diet we can hope things will get better. Note that people prone to this disease are very proud and make it difficult for anyone to get closer to them."

* * *

I told Elliott *about the conversation and he again shifted the responsibility on me by saying:*

"It's your responsibility, Pamela. You have to find the most effective way to resolve this problem. No one in the world could help Lucy better than her own mother."

Honestly, I don't understand why Elliott always transferred his responsibilities as a parent onto me. We were both parents and should have taken care of our child together.

It was difficult to believe that such a man, strong and influential in his professional field, could be such an ineffective father. In this difficult situation he was not able to face the problem and deal with it. He left everything to me.

However, we were lucky to solve this problem before it led to tragic consequences. On the recommendation of the doctor, Elliott sent Lucy to a private clinic in Switzerland specializing in eating disorders. She was a patient for six months. Elliott was transferring ten thousand dollars to the client's account each month. I prayed that everything would be okay and the problem would be solved once and for all. I felt enormous relief when Lucy came home, not completely cured, but able to cope with her condition.

* * *

She gave us a break *from her problems for the summer and we spent two easy months in our beach house in Florida.*

In September she enrolled in grade eleven classes and the nightmare started again.

Towards the end of October I got a call. On the display was the number of her school.

"Can I speak to a parent of Lucy Gerald, please," said a woman's voice.

"I'm her mother," I answered, sensing that she was about to tell me something unpleasant.

"Hi, Mrs. Gerald. I'm Pat Bradley. Lucy's math teacher. Today Lucy left school after lunch and skipped my afternoon class. Did you give written permission for her to leave school?"

"No. She doesn't have a doctor or any other appointment scheduled for today."

"There's something else. Lucy is a nice girl but lately she is not very attentive, her math grades are very low and I'm afraid she won't be able to get a credit for this class. She has changed a lot this month. She is not focused at all, her mind is somewhere else. I don't know what is going on with her, but definitely she needs to be more attentive. I encourage you to talk to her other teachers about how she is doing in their classes."

"I'll take care of this. Thank you very much for your call and your consideration."

I hung up the phone and dialed Lucy's number. The operator told me that the customer was not available at that time and to try again later. I tried a couple of times with the same result.

Where was she?

* * *

She came home at her usual after school time.

"How's school?" I asked.

"Boring, as usual."

"Your math teacher called me. She said you skipped her class. Where have you been?"

"I went to buy a new cell phone. My old one broke."

68

"Why did you have to miss your math class to buy a new phone? You could do that after school. Your father would help you as usual."

"I know what I want. I can do it myself. One math class is not a big deal."

"It is a big deal. Your teacher told me that you're not going to get your math credit as your marks are very low. What do you think you are doing? The most important thing for you is to study hard and to graduate."

"I'll pass the course."

"You better. Anyway, I need to tell your father tonight."

"Don't tell him, mom. Please. I told you I'll pass."

"Okay. I trust you. Just remember: anyone can make mistakes; some mistakes don't have big consequences, but there are mistake that can change your entire life forever."

"I'll keep that in mind. Can I go now?"

"One more thing. I need your cell to be on. I want to be able to reach you at any time. I tried to call you so many times today but I couldn't."

"My phone was dead. I told you it doesn't work."

* * *

She stopped skipping school but started coming late telling me that she was hanging out with her girlfriends.

"Do you want to go and have a mother-daughter evening together?" I asked her, assuming that maybe she needed to share something with me.

"There is nothing to talk about," she said and left. I felt as if she had slapped me in the face.

I talked to her teachers. The situation was bad. I needed to tell Elliott.

One day she didn't come home after school at all. It was almost seven when I called Elliott.

"Where are you?"

"I'm still in the bank. What's wrong?"

"I'm afraid I need to talk to you. It's an emergency, it is about Lucy."

"What about her?"

"She is not here yet."

"Did you call her?"

"She's not picking up the phone."

69

"I'm coming."

"She's with him." When he got home, Elliott showed me a scanned picture of a young man.

"Who is he?" I asked, surprised. *"And how did you find him?"*

"I logged into her Facebook account on the computer. The guys in the IT Department are good. I printed his pictures from his Facebook page while I was in the car. She has been dating this guy from more than two months. She didn't tell you?"

"I tried to talk to her, but she didn't want to share anything with me."

Elliott's cell received a message. He read it and said:

"I asked my friend in the police department to do a background check on him. He doesn't have a criminal record, but he is definitely not a proper guy for Lucy. He plays a guitar in a group at a club with a bad reputation. He may be involved in alcohol or drugs. He looks young in the picture, but he is in his early thirties."

"Oh my God! What are we going to do?"

"I will ask one of my clients in California to offer him a contract at his club. This will be an opportunity that he cannot refuse."

"That might be a good idea."

"Don't tell her anything. I will talk to her when she comes home. I hope this will work better than confronting her directly."

* * *

She came home at eleven and rushed into her room.

"Where have you been? It's almost eleven!" I said and grabbed her arm.

"Leave me alone," she answered and I smelled tobacco coming from her mouth. She rushed towards the stairs again. I yelled:

"We are not done with the conversation, young lady. Can you come down, please?"

She slammed the door of her room.

Elliott said angrily:

"I told you I'll speak with her."

"You can do that after. She needs to follow the rules we set and to show us some respect. She should come and explain to both of us why she was late. You want me to take care of her and to control her but you don't

70

respect me as a parent in her presence."

"I do respect you, but she is in difficult period of her life. You know teenagers. They are trying to find themselves. You need to understand that and be more generous."

"Her breath smells of tobacco. She should stop doing that. Take away her car and make her go to and from school with a driver who will take care of her."

"I'll go talk to her in her room."

"Whatever."

* * *

It was Christmas time when Elliott told me the guy had left the city. He visited the principal of the school and learned that Lucy had finished the semester successfully. Elliott bought her a new car as a present for her good results at school.

I was furious with him.

Now Lucy is studying in Toronto, not at Harvard, and according to Elliott it is my fault. Last night I was already in bed when he returned from his visit with Lucy in Toronto. He told me she will be under the supervision of her older cousin Robert.

* * *

Robert Gerald is Elliott's nephew, his "right hand" at the bank.

When he was only nineteen years old he got married to a club singer against the wishes of the family. Shortly after that he divorced her because he had discovered she was only after our money. That was the last time I saw him with a girl.

He lives alone in a huge apartment in an expensive condo building.

I don't think that Robert is the best person to supervise Lucy. Not only because he has had alcohol problems in the past, but it seems to me that he also likes Lucy more than as just a cousin.

When I told Elliott my concern about Robert liking Lucy more than as a cousin, he said that he would take care of it. He sent Robert to work in the Toronto branch of Gerald's bank. Now he is telling me Robert will supervise Lucy.

CHAPTER TWO

Elliott's cousin Melanie called me the next morning. She asked me if I could go to her house in the late afternoon. She wanted to talk to me about something important.

It was good to see Melanie and share with her what happened to Lucy. She is good at giving advice.

* * *

It is very important for me to look perfect every day.

I have staff that includes a stylist, hairstylist, makeup artist, and a beautician who all take good care of me. I didn't hire these people because I'm not able to take care of my beauty by myself. Not at all. I love to do things with my hands and I'm pretty good at doing makeup. But I'm lazy. After all I'm Mrs. Elliott Gerald. I buy what I want because I have money to pay for it.

If you could only see these people. How hard they work to please me. I think it is normal because they are paid very well. Some people work a month for the money they earn in a day working for me.

After I was done with all the beauty stuff I called the maid. She helped me put on the elegant green dress that I ordered from Milan.

The driver was waiting a long time for me. So what? His only responsibility was to be at my disposal.

* * *

Melanie's huge terrace was nicely decorated with flowers and small trees. She was sitting under a tent's shadow and was looking forward to hearing about her future from the taro cards.

We were about the same age but she looked like my aunt. She was wearing a wide silk robe that made her heavy body look even more rounded.

The fashion today is designed both for practicality and functionality. Most designers try to use fabrics and patterns to hide defects in female figures and to make women look more slender, tight and sexy.

Several times I offered her my help.

I told her:

"Go and talk to my personal nutritionist. He does wonders for the female figure." She strongly rejected the suggestions.

So all my efforts to make her follow a regime that would reduce her size hit a snag. One day, she even said angrily:

"Diet? Oh, you're going back to this piece of shit, Pamela. You're crazy! I'm not a model. You think I can withstand taking only tea and fruit juice. No, no. Forget it."

* * *

Melanie was so focused on her cards and didn't even notice my arrival. I approached her and said:

"Hey. How are you doing, Melanie?"

I scared her and she looked at me in surprise.

"Oh, Pamela! Hi. I was waiting for you. You look great.That dress is a work of art."

"Thank you." If I was in the mood to compliment her back and lie that she looked great I would have, but now I was too exhausted to be a well-mannered hypocrite.

"Have a seat."

"Thanks."

"Can I have a look at this clip? Come closer, please. Wow! Very nice."

"It is a set actually."

"Yeah, I can see that. What kind of stone is it? A ruby or a garnet?

"It's a ruby."

"Gorgeous set. I also love the necklace, the earrings and the bracelet. You know I'm not a jewelry person but I can appreciate this set. This colour suits your hair and your outfit. You just look amazing."

"You made my day," I said laughing. It was a miracle to get a compliment from Melanie about your appearance. She never cares how people look. That made me think that she wanted to please me before asking me for a favour.

"What are you going to drink? Coffee, tea, juice, smoothy?"

"Can I have green tea, please?"

Melanie rang for the maid and ordered green tea and biscuits.

"No sugar, please. If you have honey sweetener will be great."
I told the maid.

"You were born in September, right, so your birthstone is blue
sapphire. I think I told you that when I prepared your horoscope.
I need to look at it again; I'm not sure what your number is for this
year."

"Your horoscope was very good, Melanie. I forgot to tell you
that."

"Oh yeah? Nice to hear that."

"It was definitely helpful."

"I will prepare one for the current year with more details."

The servant served the drinks. I asked:

"Did you hear that Lucy went to study in Toronto?"

"Yeah. Robert called me in the morning."

"Elliott and I wanted her to go to Harvard, but she just left yesterday. She didn't even tell us."

"Oh my God! Lucy is such a difficult girl, so unpredictable."

"I'm telling you, it is a real trial. You witnessed all the problems she caused us. If I didn't share everything with you, I'd probably die of frustration."

"Maybe it is not as bad as it seemed in the beginning. Look at
the positive side of it. This will at least get her out of the house.
And you can finally calm down."

"From this perspective... maybe."

"Your problem is that you constantly think about it. Stop it."

"It's not all. She will be there with Robert and...."

"That's good. She won't be alone then. Robert will take care of
her."

"That's for sure but I'm a little bit scared, Melanie. I haven't
shared this with anyone but I'm scared even to say it. God, forgive
me if I'm wrong. Sometimes, I think that Robert likes Lucy. As a
woman, you know what I mean?"

She took a sip from her smoothie. There was a silence as she
was thinking about something and finally said:

"Robert is not her relative, you know that, right?"

"What? Why not?"

"You don't know? Elliott didn't tell you yet?"

"Tell me what?" I felt like a fool.

Melanie was watching me with eyes saying: "Poor woman" and put her hand on my arm.

"I told you, Elliott is a jerk. You never listen. Robert's father was adopted."

"What?"

"Robert is not a Gerald."

"How come?"

"It's a long story. Only Robert and I know the truth. Our grandfather Robert kept the secret in order to make the boy a real part of this family. In fact Ted was the son of Maggie, his first and the biggest love. I was sure Elliott told you, after he came home from Toronto. Robert told him everything yesterday. Ask him, he will tell you the whole story. I'm really surprised he didn't tell you."

I was silent for a long time.

"So, Elliott knows?"

"Yes. I told you already. Robert called me fifteen minutes ago and said he told the truth to both Lucy and Elliott."

"Unbelievable. Why didn't he tell me?"

"You stand up for Elliott all the time, but he is a real asshole."

"Melanie, what language."

"Oh come on, you know me. Listen, I want you to help me in my cause."

"Which one," I asked, as I was thinking about her astrology classes, growing flowers and her charity work in the family business.

"There is only one and it is called charity."

"What about the flowers and astrology?"

She looked at me as if I was an idiot.

"Those are just hobbies, my dear. I would advise you to forget your personal problems and be a little more involved in an activity that will benefit the poor and weak people in the community. Participation in such a noble and selfless endeavor to benefit society would bring you great joy and satisfaction. Last but not least, doing charity is profitable for the bank."

"Do you want me to participate in a charity event?"

"Kind of. It's a day program for seniors. Lately I'm interested in gerontology. I took some courses and did some volunteer work in retirement and nursing homes."

"I don't think I can do that."

"Pamela, you disappoint me."

"Don't worry, I will send a cheque."

"Sometimes money isn't the most important thing. It's also important to show compassion, empathy and support. Also, as I already told you it's all just business. It'll give the bank a good image. Every family member has already contributed; don't you think you should too? "

"Where will the event take place?"

"In a home for the elderly in Manhattan. Seniors there are very sick and I need volunteers to spend some time with them, talking, reading, empowerment, those kind of things."

"Oh, then no thanks. I'll send you a cheque."

"I don't know how much it'll cost you to go there. We'll go together if you prefer. We'll sit with them for a while and we can read a book or a magazine to them or just chat with them and then we'll leave. What do you think?"

"I don't think it's a good idea. I'm sorry Melanie but I don't like that. In the last episode of "The Bold and the Beautiful"…."

"I don't watch TV dramas," Melanie interrupted me with a cold voice. "But I can tell you that real life is far removed from the romantic and happy endings that work in your favorite soap operas."

"I think you need to respect my boundaries Melanie. I do appreciate your work helping people in need, but I just don't like to do such things. I don't want to be involved in any visits or other events. Please don't blame or judge me and accept me the way I am. Okay? Let's talk about something else."

"About what? About the last episode of "B&B"?"

"How is Margaret feeling after the flu? She scared us with that allergy reaction."

"Your mother-in-law is the most stubborn person in the world. I saw her yesterday. She is better now. But yes, she scared us to death after she took that antibiotic thing and had an allergic reaction to it. You know me, I always say that we need to go back to nature and use homeopathy and herb remedies, but she didn't listen. She almost died after taking these strong pills."

"I know. I know. She was thinking she was doing the right thing. It is good though that she is feeling well now. At her age such stress is very dangerous. Did Peter have the virus too? He was complaining about getting sick."

"My husband is such a child. Always complaining. He only had a cold and recovered fast. He is constantly busy with his business. I can barely see him lately."

"How is the real estate market after the big downturn?"

"I guess better. But there are still a lot the problems there with the mortgagees. People are losing their homes every day. At least he is quite successful."

"How did he react when Mark started working at the bank?"

"At first he was against it, of course. He wanted his son to take over the family business, but then he let him go and make his own decisions."

"And Diane? It seems to me she is very well established in the small business loans department."

"It was clear from the very beginning that she was not cut out to be an entrepreneur. She was born a bank clerk."

"Yeah. Right, right. Do they want to leave already? Young people want to live independently, in a condo downtown or close to work."

"They haven't told me of such a desire so far. I think they are okay for living here for now. But who knows? Maybe the time is not too far off."

"Are you coming to Elliott's birthday party next month?"

"Are you kidding me?"

There was nothing to say. She will hate him forever.

I left in despair.

CHAPTER THREE

"I would like to talk to you," I said with a seemingly calm voice when I got back home. He had just returned from the bank and was still in his suit. "It's important."

"Tell me, Pamela, where did we go wrong? Why did Lucy leave us? It's painful to confess, but we failed as parents."

"Why are you looking at me as if it's my fault?"

"I'm not saying that you are guilty and I'm not blaming you, but maybe you should have put in more effort to gain her trust. The best option was to become friends and she would have felt so close to you she would have shared her girlish secrets with you woman to woman."

"God is my witness; I did my best to be a good mother. I was always there for her. I just don't understand why she's ignored me all this time."

"Perhaps you didn't find the right approach."

"My approach was sincere and friendly, but she didn't want to share anything with me. It was like there was an invisible wall between us."

"It wasn't a good tactic obviously."

"Why not? Because I was pushing her to behave appropriately? Or maybe it was better to allow her to do all the stupid things she wanted to do?"

"I told you your tactics didn't work out."

"But I don't think your tactics were more successful. You strived to meet all her whims. Don't you want to understand how your behavior was wrong and how harmful it was for Lucy? Don't you understand it gave her a sense of impunity? Do you know how dangerous it could have been at her age?"

"It is my opinion that you didn't put enough effort to create a comfortable and secure environment in our home," said Elliott.

So he passed all the blame onto me again.

That hurt me deeply, but to top it off he didn't tell me about Robert. So I attacked him:

"Why didn't you tell me Robert's father was adapted?"

He shrugged.

"I'm sorry. I forgot."

"You forgot. Seriously?"

"I thought Lucy would tell you."

"No, she didn't. Neither did you."

"I said I'm sorry."

It was at that moment that I lost my temper.

"It is not enough to say you're sorry. How you can forget when you know it is important for me? You knew how worried I was about this relationship. You should have told me such an important thing. Do you know how I felt when Melanie told me? Like a fool. I don't understand how this happened between us. There is no communication at all."

"I was trying to talk to you so many times. You never listen."

"It was me who was trying to talk to you but you are always busy. Your business is so important, so obsessing. You're not the same person. I don't know you. We lost each other."

"You know that the bank is all that matters to me."

"Yes. I know that but what about me?"

"What do you mean?"

"I mean I'm sitting here alone all day. My life is empty. I'm totally ignored by my husband, by my daughter. I feel so depressed."

"Talk to your psychoanalyst about that."

"I don't want to talk to my doctor; I want to talk to you. I feel like I have been talking with doctors my whole life. I don't want to talk to doctors anymore. I want to talk to you and I'm telling you I feel very lonely."

"Perhaps I'm in a better position than you, because I have my job, but you can find a way to make your life more interesting and fulfilling. Stop watching these TV shows. Get out in society. For example help Melanie to do charity work. Recently it's very fashionable to fight for a cause like AIDS or cancer. Why not dedicate your time and efforts to the eco cause or something."

"What do you want me to do? I don't want to go naked in the streets to protect animals from slaughter or to burn a pile of fur coats?"

"I'm just giving you some ideas. Life offers so many opportunities. Enjoy the life instead of being permanently depressed."

"I'm depressed because of you and you should blame yourself. It's not my fault that the accident happened. You should have driven to that appointment twenty years ago."

He looked at me surprised.

"I was busy at the bank."

"Of course. You were so busy, as usual. If you had come to take me that day the accident wouldn't have happened."

I had never blamed him for the accident before.

The silence was heavy and ugly in that room.

Elliott took a step back.

His face was as white as a marble.

I saw his eyes full of pain, but the words had already jumped out of my mouth and nothing could take them back.

I should have stopped there, but the devil was pushing me to tell everything I was holding back all these years.

"Why were you over-parenting Lucy all these years but you never took care of me? I need your attention even more than her. It's me who is the victim of what you have done. "

I felt the satisfaction of saying what I thought for years, but not uttered aloud, because I'm not a bitch. I would not have said anything, but now he just forced me.

Elliott took another step back.

"I cannot believe you are saying that. I think it is better to go in my club and have dinner there."

"Why are you going to your club? You want to avoid the problem, don't you? Stay with me. We need to talk."

"There is nothing to talk about. You've said enough."

He left.

I was alone.

Again.

CHAPTER FOUR

*E*lliott bought *the house as a special gift for our wedding.*

We made big changes inside the building, both architecturally and in terms of functionality. Some of the rooms were converted into a swimming pool, fitness room and home theatre. However, the facade of this old building retained its original architectural style. Elliott put a lot of money into it and managed to turn this vast and cold house into our nest.

It was a combination of old and modern style, from the dusty tomes of his grandfather, neatly stacked in the library, furnished with antique furniture, to ultra-modern communication equipment and computers. We have a lot of supporting staff and servants. All of them inhabit the northern wing and in the night our floor is completely empty.

During all the years of my marriage I have lived in this chic building, like a bird in a gilded cage. For many people such a place on Fifth Avenue is a symbol of our prosperity, wealth and power.

They're right.

Elliott Gerald has all of that but it's not enough for me.

In fact I was happy in this house only during the first year of our marriage. I was Elliott's everything.

He worshiped me.

I felt loved and special.

Then all of a sudden our problems started.

* * *

I felt so miserable after Elliott left that I didn't even have any desire to watch my favorite TV shows. I went out and walked down the hallway. Then I continued down the stairs, and went to the wing looking out onto Central Park. I got to the bottom of another small hallway that led to the most beautiful and sunny part of the house. I stopped in front of one of the rooms.

I furnished and prepared this room for my future son. I asked Elliott what he thought about having another baby given that there are alternative ways. He answered:

"Are you mad? It's too late. You're thinking only about your-self as always."

Then I asked Melanie. She answered laughing at me:

"Are you mad? You have to think about menopause already, not about having babies."

I started preparing the room.

I didn't tell Elliott. He would say I was crazy.

I truly believe I will have my dream son someday.

* * *

*"**What do you want** to talk about, Mrs. Gerald," asked my psy-choanalyst when I went to see him last week.*

"I feel lost."

"Please be more specific. I need a clear picture so we can apply a suc-cessful therapy."

I didn't hesitate.

"I cannot have more children."

"But, Mrs. Gerald," said the doctor, laughing, "You have your daughter."

"I want to have more, and you know how important that is for the happiness of a family."

"Generally speaking yes, but you already have your daughter. How are the things going with your daughter lately?"

"Things could be better but, yeah, let's say it's okay so far, but there is nothing harder than being a mother of a teenager. Lucy was a very dif-ficult child, and now she has become a selfish and willful teen. I don't know, doctor, but I'm scared for my marriage. I fear for myself, because obviously I have no one to live for."

"It seems to me that giving birth is very significant importance for you. Am I right?"

"Correct."

"To understand that motherhood makes you truly happy?"

"Yes, exactly. I feel that all these years I haven't done anything other than to pretend that everything was okay and that I was really happy."

"Does your husband know about these feelings of yours?"

"He does but he thinks that I am overreacting. He has his job, though."

"What about your sex life?"

"It's kind of complicated."

"Tell me more about this."

And I told him everything. He was a good professional and didn't show any surprise nor make any judgmental comments. He was listening attentively, nodding his head to encourage me to open up and when I finished he asked:

"What do you think you should do in order to feel better?"

"I want to talk with someone about my problems, to share my feelings; also I want to have some not very strong pills in case I am very stressed so I can use them. Maybe I need to talk with my husband again."

"Which one is most important for you? Which one do you want to start with?"

"I don't know. Maybe start with the therapy."

"Alright, let's set a plan and divide it into small components. One step at a time. We will need to prepare individual program sessions. I believe that with appropriate therapy we will be able to remove the tension. Then if you still need them I will give you tranquilizers to make you feel relaxed and to free your mind of negative emotions. How does this sound to you?"

"Sounds good."

"Are you willing to try?"

"I am willing to try."

"Excellent."

"Do you think the situation can be controlled?"

"I think some things are beyond our capabilities, such as infertility for example, but when it comes to your mental health I'll work with you to resolve your issues. We will work as a team. I need your help and for you to trust in my methods."

"Thank you, doctor," I told him sincerely as I made out the cheque for his fee. *"You have given me hope that not everything is lost."*

"You are very welcome, Mrs. Gerald," he said after glancing at the cheque, and casually throwing it on his desk. *"Nurse, please make an appointment for Mrs. Gerald for the next week."*

My sessions with Dr. Milligan were very useful because I found someone with whom I could discuss my problems. This dramatically helped me cope with daily stress and he made a small fortune. I paid his high fees because I thought he absolutely deserved them. Also, I was not *used to saving money on my health.*

Unfortunately we were treating only the effects of my depression rather than its causes. I was aware that the reasons for the problems were still there and that a new conflict could arise very soon.

* * *

I turned the key and stealthily walked inside.

I lit the lamp and a bright light shone upon a lovely magic kingdom. I arranged it all myself with such pleasure and joy. I ordered all the furniture imagining how my son would play there.

I needed someone to love and need me and that person would be my son.

I took a baby blanket to cover myself and wanted to spend the night there, sad and lonely.

It was midnight when I heard Elliott coming back. I went to our bedroom very quickly as I didn't want him to look for me and find me in this room. I didn't want him to know about it yet.

CHAPTER FIVE

In the middle of December Lucy called to confirm that they were coming for Christmas. Today they were arriving and I called Lucy before she boarded the plane and told her that I would be at the airport when they arrived.

"No, mom," she said. "Don't. We will take a cab."

"I cannot wait to see you as soon as possible. I'm almost ready and the driver is here and I will be at the airport in less an hour. It will be a pleasure. Don't take that from me."

"Okay."

I told my hairdresser to brush my hair so that it would make me look younger. I put on a DK suite. It was green with a narrow skirt that ended well above the knee. I also wore a waist-length jacket that was in fashion that season. Underneath the jacket I wore a silk blouse.

I looked in the mirror and was pleased with my elegant appearance. I didn't like sports and was thankful that I did not need to do strenuous exercise or keep a strict diet to still have the figure of a girl.

As I was leaving the house I put on my new fur coat and grabbed the little black bag that complemented my suit. As it was sunny outside I also put on my dark sunglasses, just the latest fashion. I walked out of the house with confidence and gracefully got into the Cadillac Elliott gave me for Christmas. It was the latest model.

It was a beautiful afternoon. The reflection of the bright sun on the snow-covered trees made them seem magical. I felt the same way I did as a child when I had gone out to skate.

The plane arrived on time, but it was at least fifteen minutes before I saw my Lucy and Robert in the sea of arriving and departing passengers. I waved and quickly walked toward them. I felt as if I was going to faint, I was so happy to have Lucy back.

Robert was wearing a casual but elegant suit. Lucy was dressed in a mini dress and a cute pink jacket a few inches shorter than the dress. She had changed her style and she no longer looked like a raging teenager. She looked like a sophisticated young lady. Her nails which had looked like ugly shapeless claws because she bit them to the point of drawing blood were now formed in the current French manicure.

"Mom!" she said cheerfully and we hugged and I kissed her.

"Hi hon, I missed you so much."

"I missed you too."

"It is so nice to see you, Robert."

"Nice to see you, too."

I asked both:

"How are you? How was your flight?"

Robert answered:

"We are okay. The flight went really fast."

"Let's go then." I said.

We went to find the car. Robert went to find a porter to take care of the luggage.

"My God, do we have a new car?" Lucy said when she saw the Cadillac.

"Your father gave it to me as a Christmas gift."

"Cool. I like it."

The driver was holding the door open. We sat in the car and I couldn't help myself and kissed her again.

"Mom, stop it. Where is dad? I tried to call him from Toronto."

"He's at work as always. I was hoping that he would have some spare time after the company Christmas party but he is even busier. He's working every evening lately."

"I'm sure he will come for the dinner."

"You will stay for dinner Robert. Right?"

"Sure."

"We both will be staying for the dinner, mom, then we will go to Robert's condo."

I didn't say anything.

"I missed New York so much," Robert said looking at the decorated and crowded streets.

"Me too," said Lucy. "Did you finish with the Christmas shopping, mom?"

"Nope. I would really appreciate it if you can give me a hand,

Lucy."

"Not a problem"

We spent a wonderful holiday season.

The biggest gift for me was the news that Lucy and Robert were not returning to Toronto. They would be working and studying in New York.

CHAPTER SIX

Spring came early this year and the weather in March was warm and pleasant.

This morning I woke up earlier because Melanie was coming for a coffee.

I needed more time to prepare my hair, makeup and stuff. Before that I wanted to take a spa procedure and start reading the best-seller I bought yesterday.

I didn't find the book. I remembered I gave it to Elliott last night. I checked our bedroom, it wasn't there. He came late to bed and said he was reading at his office downstairs.

I assumed that maybe the book was there and went to get it.

I never go into Elliott's office. It is his territory.

The book was on his desk. It was in the plastic bag just as I gave it to him and it was obvious he hadn't even opened it.

I took it and was about to leave the room when I heard a ring.

It wasn't the home phone and the noise was coming from his jacket. I thought Elliott forgot his cell. I grabbed the jacket and started looking in his pockets. I was thinking maybe it was Elliott who was calling. I couldn't find the phone in his outside pockets and finally I saw it in one of his inside pockets.

I have never seen this phone. Did he buy a new cell phone without telling me?

I was just about to pick up when the ringing stopped.

Elliott always has a password on his phone. I didn't expect to get access to it and checked if there was a voice message. At that moment a message notice was displayed and I pushed the bottom. It wasn't password protected and I was able to read it.

It was from Elizabeth.

"Thank you for the amazing day. The necklace is gorgeous. Love you."

I read it a second time, then again and again.

He was having an affair!

Who was she?

How long?

* * *

For me it's important to respect everyone's privacy. To dig into someone's bag or pocket, to spy on someone, reading their phone or computer messages is pretty nasty. Yet, I confess I read all the messages on Elliott's phone. I felt ashamed doing so.

I wish I've never read them. In our eighteen years of marriage, I've never received such passionate massages from Elliott.

Jesus!

They'd been having a relationship for months!

I didn't know what to say or what to do.

I couldn't believe it was happening to me.

It couldn't be happening to me.

I did not have the strength to move. I felt so helpless and empty.

I pinched myself to be sure I was not dreaming.

It was a feeling as if I had been pushed off a cliff and I couldn't breathe. Suddenly my safe, orderly life was gone. It was gone.

Maybe he had some flirtations during our marriage but nothing really serious, no affair or relationship that could jeopardize our marriage.

My legs suddenly softened. I sat on his chair. It seemed as if I had disappeared from the world. I didn't know how long I was in Elliott's office when a servant told me that Melanie had arrived.

When she saw me with my hair undone and no makeup, she exclaimed:

"Pamela. What's wrong?"

I looked at her with empty eyes and said:

"Elliott's having an affair."

Then I looked at her face and - oh my God! The bitch already knew about it!

"Why you didn't tell me?"

"I didn't want to be involved in this situation."

"I thought you were my friend."

"I'm, but I didn't want to be the one to tell you that Elliott will be asking for divorce."

"Divorce? Is it that serious already?"

"People are saying it is. I'm so sorry, Pamela"

"People? Of course. I'm the last one to learn about it."

"Did Elliott tell you finally?"

"No, I found out by chance. I saw their messages on his cell."

"Oh, my God!"

"Who is she?"

"She works in the bank."

"Okay?"

"She's an ambitious young bitch."

"How young?"

"Twenty-five or twenty-seven or something."

"Twenty? She's the same age as of our daughter!"

"Yes. What a shame. Diane told me it's not a secret in the bank."

"When did it start?"

"Diane told me it was after the company Christmas party."

"It's been that long and he didn't tell me anything! If I didn't go into his office I would be the only one that doesn't know Elliott is cheating on me."

Melanie said:

"I know, my dear, I know. There is no bigger coward and villain than the unfaithful husband."

"I am sorry, Melanie, for cancelling our coffee, but I'm going to the bank."

"Don't do that. Please, Pamela. Talk to him when he comes home."

"I need to talk to him now."

"Don't do anything stupid."

"It's not me who is being stupid. Now, if you excuse me, Melanie I'm going."

I instructed the driver to be ready in fifteen minutes, then I put on some jeans and a sweater and left.

Security guards at the bank's lobby greeted me politely but I answered with a cold nodding.

Florence - Elliott's secretary looked like she was seeing a ghost when I opened the door of the CEO office. She was completely shocked and didn't try to hide it. Melanie was right; they all know about his affair.

"Mrs Gerald. Good afternoon."

"I want to see my husband immediately."

"He's at a meeting. I'll call him and tell him that you are here. Do you want something to drink?"

I didn't answer and walked across the room intending to enter Elliott's office.

"Mrs Gerald, please," she said, scared, but she didn't try to stop me.

Smart woman!

I looked at her. During all the years she had worked for Elliott I knew she was beautiful but with my instincts I felt that she was not a threat to my marriage.

I opened the door. Elliott wasn't there. I heard voices coming from the conference room. The door was open so I went in. I saw three men sitting just in front of me. They stopped talking and stared at me.

"Pamela? What's wrong?" Elliott jumped and looked at me scared. "Is Lucy okay?"

"It's not about Lucy. I need to talk to you. It's an emergency."

"Can you wait in my office for a moment? We're almost done."

"Right now." I said emphatically.

"Gentlemen will you excuse me? I will inform you by email regarding my final decision."

They left in silence.

"You forgot this. Also you forgot to give me the number of your new cell." I said when the last one closed the door.

He looked shocked, although he made an effort to hide it.

"Where did you find it? I thought I lost it."

"It's safe. Don't worry. It was in the deepest pocket of your jacket."

"Listen...."

"I know everything. I cannot believe you did this to me," I yelled and threw the cell on the floor.

"Pamela, please. The bank is not the place for this kind of conversation. I'll explain everything. If you want to talk right now let's go home."

He grabbed my hand.

"Don't touch me! I'm not such a stupid woman to listen to your explanation. I want to know how you'd dare to...."

"It was nothing, trust me."

"It appears there is something."

He interrupted me, scared.

"Please, lower your voice. There are clients. Let's talk as mature people and solve our problems as adults. Do you want some water?"

He went to the other corner of the room to fill a glass of water.

"I don't care about your bank. I don't care about your clients. Do you want me to go out of this office and to tell them how amoral Elliott Gerald is? Do they know that you are a liar or maybe they already know?"

I rushed to the door and didn't see Elliott run across the room. He jumped on me in order to stop me. His arm hit my chin very hard. I lost balance, cracked my head on the edge of his desk and then fell on the floor unconscious.

* * *

After a couple of minutes I regained consciousness, but it was enough time for Elliott to pick me up and take me to the staff elevator. When I opened my eyes I saw we were already in the garage.

"To the New York Hospital," he said to the driver.

"I don't want to go to hospital. I want to go home."

I couldn't feel my head. The pain was incredible.

"It could be dangerous. You fell really badly."

"Because you pushed me," I thought but didn't say anything.

I closed my eyes and we arrived in silence.

The hospital was crowded. I hate hospitals. They make me anxious.

"She fainted and hit her head," he said in the emergency department.

"Has she been unconscious?" the doctor asked.

"Yes."

"How long?"

Elliott hesitated for a second.

95

"I don't know exactly but it wasn't long, a couple of minutes."

"How did the injury happen?"

"She just slipped on the floor and hit her head on the edge of the desk."

Such a liar!

After an examination the doctor said:

"You're lucky, Mrs Gerald. You have suffered a concussion. Fortunately it is not a severe one, so there won't be serious effects to your health."

"Thank God," said Elliott. "Should she stay in the hospital for further examinations?"

"No, not at all. We have done the necessary examination and there is no indication of serious trauma, brain damage, or neck injury. A hematoma is common and will go away on its own with time. The use of ice may help decrease its size. You can go home, Mrs Gerald and take it easy for couple of days. Complete rest. Avoid worrying."

"Is it possible that she may have some problems later? Does she need any medication?"

"She needs to stay in bed for a while because she might feel dizzy. Bed rest, fluids, and a mild painkiller. Ice, as I said, may be applied to bumps to relieve pain and decrease swelling."

"Thanks doctor," Elliott said

"You're very welcome, sir. Just doing my job. There is one more thing. We provide initial treatment here but a follow-up will be required. I'll refer you for a follow-up to your family doctor. Make an appointment with your family doctor who may suggest you see a specialist, such as a neurologist."

"Sure," Elliott nodded.

"It's important to keep these appointments, particularly because some of the more subtle problems associated with concussions such as memory deficits, personality changes, and changes in cognition may not be apparent at the time of the initial injury."

"We'll do that," Elliott nodded again.

"If you don't have any other questions go to the reception desk and ask for a printout of the findings of the examination. It will only take a few minutes for me to update your hospital file to include these findings. Give the printout to your family doctor."

In the car Elliott told me:

"Pamela, I'm so sorry. I'm such a stupid man. Please, forgive me. I swear, I will stop seeing this woman. "

I didn't say anything and he continued:

"I didn't want to hurt you, trust me. I'll do whatever you want, just tell me, Pamela, say something…please…."

But I was numb.

CHAPTER SEVEN

I **fell into a depression** as deep as the one after the accident twenty years ago and spent more than a month in my bed. I started taking Prozac again. The pills made me relaxed and somehow alive.

I didn't want to see Elliott.

I was sure he had hit me on purpose.

I didn't want to see my family doctor or my psychotherapist.

Lucy was calling me every day. She was the only person I talked to.

* * *

As I realized that I was losing Elliott I suddenly became aware of the fact that I loved him more than ever.

Even the thought that he could leave me was causing me physical pain.

I liked everything about him now, even the things I didn't like before. For example I was annoyed that he wasn't tall enough, and only a few inches taller than me. But now I found that very sexy. He has subtle but strong bones, and was wonderfully muscled. He keeps his muscles toned by swimming regularly in our pool. He transformed the entire north side of the house into a huge gym with a sauna and massage room. He spends at least an hour every morning there.

* * *

I was at my next session of psycho-relaxation with music when I decided to share my new problem with Dr. Milligan:

"I'm afraid that there are new problems that threaten to strain the relations with my husband."

"What exactly are they?" he asked me.

"I'm haunted by constant sexual desire that torments me. I constantly dream about having sex, but Elliott barely notices me. He doesn't even touch me, hug me, or kiss me. I miss this intimacy."

"And when you're together, do you try to hug him, to kiss him?"

"We are not really together lately. He comes home late every night and says he has been working in the office. I believe he really does work there sometimes, because he used to work late before, but in most cases I'm sure he is going to see the other one."

"He promised to stop seeing her, right?"

"Yes, but I'm not sure he did and it makes me suffer."

"What do you think you should do?"

"Me? I can do what he did and have an affair myself."

"Do you really believe that will make you feel better about your husband's affair?"

"Not really, I have my dignity and pride. I can't just offer and sell myself."

"What do you mean by that?"

"Well…there are many discrete ways, you know, but…."

"I'm listening."

"No, no. Elliott is the meaning of my life. I don't want another sexual partner."

"Have you talked with your husband again about trying some of the latest methods of having a baby?"

"I did, but he gave me the same answer. He said it was too late and he doesn't want to go through the whole process."

"Did you tell him how important it is for you?"

"Oh, yeah but he said that I am selfish and I am thinking only about myself."

"How did you feel when he said that?"

"I felt disappointed in him. I was hurt so badly."

"You felt disappointed and hurt because…."

"Because he actually betrayed me and our marriage. Maybe he doesn't love me anymore. I don't know. It might also be because of this woman. If she wasn't in his life he would be more concerned about me and what is important for me. He was fulfilling all my wishes until he became involved with her."

"What we can do in such cases is to think as little as possible about negative emotions and experiences. Now relax and listen to the music," he said as he put his hands on my forehead. "The most important thing to understand is what is happening in our lives. Think about the good things."

I was lying on the couch and as he massaged my temples while the soft music played I felt my body relax as he kept saying:

"Imagine that you are a child, a little innocent child. No problems, you have no heartache. Strong light surrounds your face; warmth is spilling on your body. You are a little innocent child...."

CHAPTER EIGHT

Next week will be Elliott's birthday. Every year we plan a magnificent party. To this event we invite the elite of Wall Street, investors, bankers, politicians, all the members of our family and all our friends.

The press will be given limited access, only reputable news channels, newspapers and magazines.

This birthday is a jubilee. Elliott is turning fifty.

I have hired a specialized firm to organize the party, but the idea of the theme, menu and the arranging was entirely my doing.

Keeping myself busy organizing the party I forgot for a moment about my problems and concerns.

"Pamela, are you okay?" cousin Anna asked me when all the guests had arrived for Elliott's birthday and the party was in full swing.

"Yes. Of course. Why?"

"Because you're so pale. Do you want something to drink, maybe a glass of water?"

"I'm fine. Perhaps the excitement makes me dizzy, but I'm good," and I hurried to get away from her. I was feeling worse than ever, because in the hall a young girl had entered, and was talking to Elliott. From the way he was looking at her I realized it was that woman.

My God, how dare Elliott to invite her into our house! On his birthday! I was the one who organized everything perfectly for his jubilee. And how does he repay me?

By bringing his lover.

She didn't have the right to be here.

I looked at her with the eye of a woman who is evaluating her rival. She wasn't beautiful but had charm and something that I myself had never had: a nice, round and sexy body. Her hair was black and falling freely over the shoulders. The ultra-modern dress of black lace was simple but provocative.

Did Elliott buy her this unique dress from some expensive

boutique?

It wasn't important to me now. The real problem for me was that the dress was covering the vibrant and strong body of a woman who was much younger than me.

My first thought was to rush to them and separate them.

Then I wanted to ask Elliott how he had the audacity to show off his mistress in front of everybody.

But I couldn't do anything to express my indignation.

I couldn't slap Elliott in front of the guests, nor could I grab the woman and eject her from the party.

I had no right to cause a scandal, even though I was in my own house.

I realized that I had never been so cruelly humiliated. I refused to believe my eyes, but they stood before me, so absorbed in each other that they did not even notice that I was watching them.

Maybe Elliott would officially present Her Majesty to me.

I was so afraid that this could really happen, so, in a panic I grabbed a drink from a passing waiter and quickly went into the garden. Escaping the guests I hid behind a bush and sat on the little bench beside it. I drank the whole glass of wine in one gulp, trying not to cry.

I knew that this woman existed, but I didn't expect that he would cause me such an embarrassment by bring her into our home. When I thought about how much effort I put into his party just to make him happy I wanted to kill them both. I felt sorry for myself. How naive and stupid I was.

I was dedicated to organizing this party as only a desperate and abandoned spouse could be. It was like trying to glue a broken vase and pretend it had not been broken. While I was thinking how to arrange the rooms, how to pick the menu and drinks I was trying to believe that I was still the lady of the house.

I hired a gourmet specialist to recommend the food and the order of servings. He described nine different meals to be combined with appropriate drinks - first roast lamb, second eggs, then lobster, duck, veal, and fruits. I wanted everything to be perfect and this party to become a real event. Honestly speaking I was trying to convince myself that I was better than the other woman and

Elliott would be smart enough to see that.

I spent a fortune to look stunning. I visited all the expensive boutiques to choose the right dress and accessories. Finally, my stylist advised me to choose a Valentino dress. We liked this model when we attended his preview. It was bright red, sat tightly on the body and was perfectly suited to my figure and my hair. I don't have big boobs so I ordered a new bra, a special cut "Victoria's secret" that successfully corrected what I was not given by nature.

I thought I had done everything I could do to be the most wonderful hostess of an event of this kind.

I was hoping to read in the media how cleverly I organized a truly world-class party.

I hoped Elliott would be happy with how I dealt with the difficult task of being a perfect Mrs. Elliott Gerald, but alas.

I wanted to be alone for a while. I needed to suppress my feelings of despair and hide them behind my usual mask of happiness. Then, guided by some innate sense of duty I stood up and went inside. Nobody had noticed my absence, so I decided to go to my room and fix my makeup. I got on the beautiful, luxurious internal elevator. It led directly into my boudoir.

My walk-in closet was big and well organized by the servants - wardrobes, removable hangers and shelves filled with different patterns and colours of shoes.

I looked into the mirror of my dressing table. I saw a face of a scared woman. Then my eyes slid down to the table all covered with makeup and beauty products.

I opened one of the drawers where I kept a small part of my high end jewelry.

I reached out and took one of the boxes. It was a set of diamond necklace, dangling earrings and a cuff bracelet. Diamonds were shining in all of their glory. Elliott told me that it's a unique handmade set and it's worth a small apartment, but right now the beauty of the stones seemed repulsive.

I enjoyed receiving these precious jewels in the past only because it was a sign of my husband's love.

He didn't love me anymore. If he did he would not have brought his mistress into my home. Elliott just announced to the New York's elite that he cares more for her than for his wife.

I opened the other drawers and looked at all the rings, pendants, necklaces, gold and platinum pins. There was my collection of watches. One watch was inlaid with diamonds and emeralds and cost a small fortune.

My God!

So beautiful but so useless and unnecessary.

Just like myself....

I looked around and felt my life slipping away.

I had everything a woman could want: money, a luxurious life, expensive clothes and jewelry.

What was I missing?

Happiness, of course.

My life had passed in this luxurious house, in this posh room, among all these unnecessary expensive items. I needed more than that. I needed warmth and affection, love and attention.

I felt a desire to destroy all the expensive jewelry, to destroy all the luxuries that surrounded me. What was the sense of having all these beautiful things when my soul was empty, when my husband didn't love me?

Nobody needed me!

If so, I would end all this.

But I didn't have the strength to do it. I didn't dare destroy everything unnecessary, everything fake.

Instead I went into the bathroom.

Refreshed a little.

Applied new makeup.

Took a double dose of tranquilizers and returned to the battlefield.

I was smiling, but the pain inside me was killing me. I tried to hide it behind a fake smile and confidence.

"What's wrong, Pamela?" Oliver, Elliott's brother, asked me, when I came into the room and ran into him.

He always looked good and elegant. He took good care of himself, but the dark circles and swollen skin under the eyes revealed his alcohol abuse.

I was terrified. Was it so obvious?

"Everything's fine."

"You look stunning as always, Pamela."

"Thanks a lot, Oliver." I couldn't completely hide my tension.

"Relax, all right?" The party is going great."

"I'm giving my best."

"Do you want a drink?" Oliver asked me sympathetically.

I nodded because I wasn't able to speak.

I always thought that Oliver was not only the most handsome but also the most decent of Elliott's brothers.

We went to the bar and I took a glass of wine. It's dangerous to drink when taking antidepressants, but I drank the wine in one gulp. Maybe it's better to die.

"Oh, Oliver." I sobbed, but made an effort to hold back the tears.

"Problems with Elliott, right?"

"You know we have had problems for a long time but just recently it's become intolerable."

"Did you ever think about divorce?"

"No...never...but I'm not sure about Elliott."

He didn't look surprised. This betrayer - Elliott. He had already told Oliver about his plans to divorce me.

"I hate Elliott's dirty games, Pamela. Especially when he plays them on you."

"I've never been in such a dead-lock before."

Oliver took another drink. Then said:

"My life is a real mess too. You know, after our older son died in Afghanistan I felt empty. Then Eddy becomes an actor instead of joining the family business. I am so disappointed, so lost."

I felt strange. We were both frightened and despaired for our lives. I felt relieved; as if Oliver had taken a piece of my grief and made my pain smaller.

"Oh, Oliver," I exclaimed again, but he didn't hear me.

"What are you waiting for," he told me as he gazed somewhere behind my back. He was probably watching Elliott. "Why aren't you taking action? You can change things in your favor. Why should you sit all day in this huge, empty house? Go and live as you deserve."

"What do you want me to do? "

"If the other party is intolerant, I don't understand why you have scruples, and continue to be faithful."

"Pamela, such a great party," a voice said behind me. I turned
and saw Melinda Berg, one of the lovers of Jason Fearbank, a
friend of Elliott. "Congratulations, my dear."

"Thanks, dear Melinda."

I was wondering how to get rid of Melinda when I saw Bill
Barrymore, one of the most prominent photographers of New
Yorker Today.

"Mrs. Gerald would it be convenient for you to take the pictures now?"

"Of course," I said with a grin while thinking: "Picture. That's
exactly what I need right now. God help me."

"Could you excuse me for a moment," I told Oliver and
Melinda before going with Barrymore.

"I hope it won't take much time because I cannot leave my
guests."

It was another challenge that I need to survive this endless
night. I thought about Oliver's words. However, I didn't have a
choice. I had to play my role to the very end of this show.

"Not at all. About fifteen minutes. My assistants have found
the right place."

Barrymore had made a fortune selling pictures and was working with a team of several young boys who were already carrying
cables, cameras and projectors. He promised not to take a long
time, but it was more than half an hour before I finished posing.

I thought Elliott might ask for me, so I sent the head butler to
tell him I was in the library. When I returned, the party was in full
swing. Nobody suffered from my absence. The fun would continue in full force until the morning, but for me the celebration was
already over.

I looked around to find Elliott but I couldn't see him any-
where. I even checked the garden but I didn't see him. Neither did
I see the girl.

Where was Elliott?

CHAPTER NINE

Several days later, the butler brought me the mail and pile of letters. Among the magazines I saw the cover of *The New Yorker Today*. I threw a casual glance at my picture. I was not excited. It wasn't my first portrait. I have posed for various magazines many times before.

Now, my attention was grabbed by something that I hadn't seen in my previous pictures.

I found terrifying changes in the expression on my face. A new, unknown woman in her forties was staring at me from the cover page of the magazine. But I'm not forty yet. Not yet.

The daily care of cosmetics weren't able to stop time. I was wondering how that was possible.

I never saw the signs of fatigue and maturity during the long hours I spent in front of the mirror, while doing my hair and putting on my makeup.

I stayed still for a long, long time with the magazine in my hands, continuing to stare at my face, an image known and unknown to me, a woman who was Pamela Gerald and at the same time definitely wasn't me.

Readers of *The New Yorker Today* would probably see on this cover one beautiful well-kept woman. No double chin, no shadows under the eye, no sagging skin. Perfect makeup. I've probably managed to outsmart others, but I couldn't lie to myself. I realized, horrified, that the sparkle in my eyes had already gone. While looking at the picture I wondered if I still had a passion for life in my soul.

After I saw this picture I developed a new obsession. I started constantly monitoring my face. I tried to discover any new evidence of aging and to convince myself that I was becoming old.

Oh, God!

It was ridiculous!

I was sometimes spending the whole morning observing my face. Every time I looked in the mirror I found a new wrinkle.

* * *

"I looked at the mirror one morning and I couldn't recognize myself," I told the only person willing to listen to me, my psychiatrist.

"All of us sooner or later are going into middle and late adulthood," he told me tactfully. "Unfortunately it's absolutely true. Usually we realize it suddenly. That's why we are so shocked."

"I'll be forty soon. Am I becoming old, doc?" I asked naively, expecting him to deny it. I was paying him a fortune to give me answers I wanted to hear.

"People in their forties aren't old, Pamela, but they are also not teens. It is difficult for many patients to make transitions in their life, but for those in middle adulthood it is very important to keep perspective in their life. For you, for example, it will be in big advantage to maintain your sense of motivation and optimism. A woman like you should have all the prerequisites for optimism."

"I thought that aging was for others, but not for me." I rushed to pour out my soul. "As if suddenly I woke up and felt that I could not stop the time."

"We all do. Have you ever met people you haven't seen in a long time? When we see that they are no longer young, we know we've also changed significantly since we were young."

"No, no. I don't feel ready to stand on the threshold of old age. I'm not ready."

* * *

There was no doubt - life had slipped between my fingers and I hadn't even begun to live.

I had nothing.

I was married to a man who swore he loved me but at the same time he wasn't sleeping with me and was having a mistress.

Lately he didn't even notice me at all. Probably never thought that he was obliged for the years in which I served his cause and played the role of a perfect wife. Now he doesn't even want to know that I needed attention and affection.

From such a man you can hardly expect gratitude for having

wasted your life because of him. So many important things have passed by me without my experiencing them, just because I was wholly committed to him.

I was sorry for all the missed opportunities. I realized that now more than ever I needed someone to love and respect me.

I had to get it now because time flies by quickly and ruthlessly and it would be too late very soon.

I am not going to wait for a man to make me his lover. I would find the guy.

I remembered clearly Oliver's words: "Elliott doesn't understand you, and he doesn't appreciate you. Find another man who will accept with gratitude the enormous love and tenderness that you have in your heart. Love makes you feel alive. If you don't take care of yourself no one will do it for you. Do it, Pamela. Do it now because later it will be too late."

I was going to listen to his advice.

Elliott would pay for all the suffering that he caused me.

Sooner or later he would pay.

I definitely would take care of it.

PART THREE

ELLIOTT

CHAPTER ONE

It's difficult to believe I'm turning fifty.

When I was very young, I thought that people in their fifties were boring, picky seniors who had crossed the threshold into old age. The thought of being around someone who was half a century old gave me creeps.

It seemed that at that age there would be no more pleasures and challenges. Just the very end of your life.

But today, on my 50th birthday, I realize how wrong I was. On this warm Saturday evening, I feel I'm still young and strong and I have my whole life ahead.

Assessing my life so far, I can be happy and proud of my accomplishments. I have money, power and influence.

Tonight my high position in society can be seen by the variety of guests that have come to my birthday party. Politicians, diplomats, royals, captains of industry, bankers, lawyers, celebrities, entertainment executives and journalists.

Tonight, at my home, I can see the cream of New York society. I can see fine gentlemen and ladies with elegant costumes and dresses. There are also good-looking young men and women with athletic figures, modeled with diligence and perseverance in the gyms.

Years ago when I bought this house, I had a special ballroom built that could accommodate two hundred people. All of the two hundred special guests invited are here tonight. It took Pamela and me more than an hour to welcome the guests and accept their congratulations and the gifts. I could not open the gifts at the party, but knowing the financial status of most of the guests, the value of the gifts will be quite impressive. Some might say that I'm greedy, but I'm just a man of business.

When Pamela told me how much the party would cost I immediately started looking for ways to pay for it.

I really have a flair for making money.

I signed a contract with the magazine *New York Banking News,* which paid an impressive price for the exclusive rights to cover the entire celebration. Other media's representatives, who were invited in advance, were entitled to take protocol pictures only.

The deal was signed at the last moment. I told Pamela about it the night before the party. She wasn't very impressed. I know she does not understand or appreciate the pleasure I get out of making money.

I like to use other's money to pay for even my private expenses and on the top of it to make a profit.

Adding to that the respect and celebrity that I will reap, as this celebration will be certainly the main event of the year, the result would be double. Advertising is always necessary.

Pamela did a great job organizing the party.

The marble hall and the large bright mirrors are festively decorated with streamers and balloons. The entire garden shines under the lights of countless coloured lights. The company that Pamela hired to cater the party sent a dozen nimble waiters who are constantly restocking tables with gourmet food and drinks.

Indeed, everything has been done perfectly. I thanked Pamela, after all the toasts and congratulations. I asked her to be my partner for the first dance. This dance is important because not only will we be the first people on the dance floor, but the guests will also know that the dance floor is open. I had hired a popular band to entertain the guests. For those who didn't like this kind of music and for young people a DJ was in the garden.

My bodyguards were around taking care of my safety and the safety of my guests.

Although almost all the invitees have already arrived and the party was well underway, I was nervous.

I still hadn't seen my nephew John. He had to have come with Elizabeth. This woman was my mistress at one time, but she has taken on a more serious and important role in my life.

In the beginning it was nothing more than sex. I was absolutely sure she was completely indifferent to me and always would be. She was an employee in the bank. One of these ambitious young bitches wholly devoted to the work and the career. This kind of girl is very far removed from serious commitments and relationships.

She was exactly the partner I needed at that moment. Always

at hand. It was so convenient.

This situation was in tune with my plans to have an affair and nothing more than that.

But....

But in one certain moment, I cannot say exactly when, my feelings for this woman changed dramatically. I realized that I had fallen in love with her as strongly as only a fifty year old man could.

* * *

Someone interrupted my thoughts and I turned to see who was speaking.

"Such a great evening, Elliott," said Tim Hammond, my partner and client.

"Thanks," I said.

"I believe this will be one of the events of the year and will be talked about for a long time. By the way, what happened with that project for scientific research I sent you?"

"I called the dean of the university and got all the details on the projects."

"Are you going to support them?" asked Tim.

"The Governing Council decided yesterday to donate twenty million dollars to the university".

I looked at him to see his reaction. He was impressed and said:

"Very noble and profitable."

"I think so," I agreed.

"When will this investment return?"

"I think it'll be sooner than I initially expected."

"Sounds great!" He was a billionaire but even didn't try to hide the greedy sparkle in his eyes.

"I ordered my staff to transfer half of the amount we had agreed. Your percentage of the deal."

"It's a pleasure to work with you, Elliott."

"The feeling is mutual," I said politely and was just about to ask for some confidential information about his company when John and Elizabeth showed up.

She looked stunning. She was wearing the fantastic dress I

117

had bought for her. A special gift for this special evening. It was crazy to push John to bring my mistress here. I completely understand that. However it was an important day of my life and I wanted her to be with me.

"Excuse me, Tim, but new guests just came in. We'll talk later."

"Sure, sure." Thanks for the invitation and for the business."

* * *

John looked nervous. So did Elisabeth.

"Happy Birthday!" John said.

"You look great!" I told Elizabeth, and forgot to answer John's salutation. He stood for a moment wondering what to do and then went to the bar.

"Why didn't you put on the gift that I gave you?"

I also bought her high-end jewelry to match her new outfit. I chose a classic collection of a necklace, bracelet and earrings with white and yellow sapphires and diamonds set in a gold background.

"I've never worn such expensive jewelry in my life. I was scared something might happen. At the last minute I gave up."

"What can happen to them? You're among some of the richest men in America."

"I know, but I'm just not used to it."

"Don't worry. We will have enough opportunities for you to put them on."

"You're so nice, Elliott."

"I just got a new Cessna, a gift to me for my birthday. I plan for you and me to be the first passengers."

"Oh, Elliott!"

"In fact I bought it for us. To be at our disposal at any time."

After this conversation I had to avoid paying Elizabeth any more attention. I didn't want people to comment on that.

Glancing around the room, my eyes stopped on Pamela.

She looked like a woman who was in her second youth. It is obvious that her beauty was the result of a lot of effort and money. Pamela looks great for her age; no doubt. But if she stood next to Elizabeth, there would be no comparison.

Elizabeth's freshness is like the sweet nectar of a great juicy peach, while my wife is the overripe beauty of a hot but already passing late summer. Even the best brand of cosmetics cannot hide the ravages of time on Pamela's skin. Very soon the day will come when she might seek the help of a good plastic surgeon.

The special, expensive bra that Pamela is wearing could probably deceive others. But I know that her bust is not as perfect and full as it seems. Her boobs are really small. Although, I liked them a long time ago, now this lack of oomph is just stirring my boredom and a desire to be with the other.

My eyes go back to Elizabeth. She is so sensual and seductive. She never makes an effort to please anyone and that is perhaps the magic of her impact on me, and perhaps on the other men. It is difficult to explain, but I feel it with all my male nature.

* * *

If I don't count the short-term relationships, I have loved only two women in my life. It seems to me that my love for Elizabeth will probably have very serious consequences for us all.

I don't know why, but things in my life are always arranged in a very dramatic way. I met my wife Pamela at a charity dinner hosted by her father, the wealthy banker Kevin Fletcher.

It was fate.

It was destiny.

When he presented her, I immediately decided that she would become my wife. She was thin and airy with beautiful, naturally blonde hair and beautiful high cheekbones. She possessed a real fine porcelain figurine. She also stood and looked at me as if hypnotized. Her eyes had became enormous.

We began to meet and I married her after just a couple of months. I got a call at the bank when she was pregnant with our first child.

* * *

Police were looking for me.

I was told that Pamela had been in a car crash.

"How did it happen?" I asked.

"A cab hit her car. She was in the back seat, otherwise it would have been far worse," said the policeman.

"Where is she now?"

"The Hunter Hospital."

"Thank you for calling," I said and hung up the phone.

"What is it?" asked me my brother Ted who was in the room at that moment.

"It was the police. Pamela has been in a car crash," I said, terrified.

"This is terrible. How is she?"

"She is in the hospital."

"What about the baby?"

I swallowed painfully before saying:

"The officer didn't say anything about it," I said with a dry mouth. "I have to go to the hospital."

"I would like to go with you, if you don't mind."

"Okay. Thanks Ted."

* * *

The lobby of the hospital was full and crowded. Some people were carrying flowers and gifts; others were hurrying to the elevator worried. A nurse was putting a patient in a wheelchair and two other nurses were talking animatedly at the reception. Right in front of me a pregnant woman slowly passed with an intense expression of fear on her face. The husband, who looked even more scared, was carrying her bag.

"Calm down, dear," he said hurriedly. "Everything will be okay. Walk carefully. What is it?"

The woman clutched her stomach.

"It starts! My God, it begins!"

"We are almost there. Relax sweetheart. We arrived already." The man spoke soothingly, but his voice was trembling and obviously he would need help himself very soon.

I rushed to the reception.

"Where can I find my wife Pamela Gerald? She was in a car accident. She'is pregnant."

"She is in the Emergency. The Doctor will be with you shortly."

Ted and I sat in the waiting room.

I thought I would die of fear.

120

How was she?

How was our baby?

"Just calm down, Elliott," said Ted. "There is nothing that we can do except pray."

"How is she, Doctor?" I asked when he finally came to talk to us.

"You are the husband, right?"

"Yes, I'm Pamela Gerald's husband."

"I'm sorry, Mr. Gerald, but it was a bad crash. The labour started prematurely and now we have to fight for the lives of both."

"What are the chances?"

"She has lost a lot of blood. Let's pray for a good outcome."

* * *

After more than an hour which felt like a century he returned.

"Congratulation, you have a daughter, Mrs. Gerald. The baby came earlier but will be okay. I'm sorry but we had to remove the genital organs of your spouse. Unfortunately she will no longer be able to have children. But given that her life was saved, and you have this wonderful girl, things have evolved in a relatively good way."

"The most important thing is that they both are saved and will be fine. Thank you so much."

"It's our duty," he tapped me on the shoulder sympathetically.

"Can I see them?"

"Currently Mrs. Gerald is having some additional treatments, but then you can see them. Please, no more than a minute."

"Yes, of course."

* * *

After a while, the nurse came to call me.

As she was lying on the hospital bed Pamela looked frail as a child. There were no signs of head injuries, but one arm was bandaged and the other attached to an IV. Her face was very pale, and almost blended into the colour of the pillow. With her eyes closed, she looked dead.

The nurse gave me a sign to leave.

"Can I see my daughter please? Just for a second."

She nodded.

121

*We went through another corridor and into the room were the new-
borns were kept. The nurse introduced me to my daughter.*

She was so small.

I was scared.

*My heart stopped. I realized how fragile life is and how we can lose
everything in just a second.*

* * *

"Happy birthday, papa, our apologies for being late," interrupted my thoughts as Lucy rushed towards me and put her arms
around my neck. Behind her was Robert.

"You know me. I never come on time."

Upon their return from Paris, last month, Lucy began persistently calling me "papa."

"I thought Robert would make you more precise and organized."

"Oh, he failed…." Lucy burst out.

"Papa, I brought you a special gift from Paris, but I'll give it to
you when we are alone. It's very special."

"Let me introduce you to Elizabeth Worry."

"Hi, Elisabeth," said Robert.

"How are you, Elisabeth?" Lucy asked.

"I'm fine, thanks."

"Forgive me, but I'm thirsty. Honey, let's go to the bar. Or even
better let's eat first. Bye, papa, see you later. It was nice to meet
you, Elizabeth." Finally Lucy stopped chirping.

They left.

"I was expecting that," Elizabeth said almost crying. "I want to
go home."

"Stop it. Lucy doesn't know about us."

"But Robert does."

"Let's drink something. I'll introduce you to some people in
the banking field and then I will get my driver to drive you home.
Then I also will come."

It was past midnight when the driver drove me to Elizabeth's
apartment I had bought for her. I chose a large maisonette, close to
the bank so I would be able to visit her after work. Sometimes, we

122

went there even during the day. I stayed with Elizabeth for about an hour and I would have loved to stay until morning, but she insisted on my going back to the party.

"You need to go back to the party. Don't forget that you are the host, and your favorite reporters are looking for you," she said.

"They can go to the hell."

"What about your guests?"

"Be sure that all have forgotten about me. The party has reached the stage when all are properly drunk."

"That probably does not apply to everyone. For example, Pamela"

"Yes, that's true."

I got out of bed and quickly dressed. The driver brought me back home. Pamela really was the only one who noticed my absence. She pulled me aside.

"Where have you been?"

"I went out to get a little fresh air." I tried to look as innocent as possible.

"Do you really think that I'm blind? Or naive? You were missing almost two hours."

"Why are you so angry, Pamela? Do you think anyone noticed my absence?"

"You know what? It is just too much. I think that it is the pinnacle of arrogance to invite the most influential people in the city on your birthday, then to bring your mistress and to introduce her as if she is one of us. On top of that you leave your own party just to go and have sex with this bitch. This is simply outrageous."

"Who cares about all that?"

"Your behavior is more than rude. You have no right to bring this woman into my house."

"Pamela, what's wrong with you?"

"What's wrong with me? I've the right to forbid you to show up with your mistress in public. If you don't stop seeing this woman, I swear to God I'll destroy you both. You can't imagine what I might be able to do if someone humiliates me."

Her eyes looked as if they were throwing sparks and I was scared of the hate I read there.

Suddenly her anger left her, her eyes changed. Their expres-

sion of overt hostility was gone and she smiled radiantly to someone. The Stags, one of the richest families in New York was
approaching to say goodbye.

One reporter diligently was taking pictures. Pamela's poses
were almost professional. What smiles, what playful looks.

God, what hypocrisy. I had never imagined that my wife had
such artistic talent. Even I, a good player, could not give a better
performance.

CHAPTER TWO

I **go to the office** no later than nine am. I am totally devoted to what I am doing and require the same devotion from my employees. During the long years I have spent in the bank I realized that setting a personal example is very important, so the rules imposed by me were binding for everyone, especially me.

It was me who made the family business one of the most prosperous in the world. As of January 30, 2015, the company's assets totalled $400 billion with a market capitalization of $30.4 billion. Today the company is well known as a reputable institution in investment management and investment services. The Gerald Bank's clients are influential people, corporations and governments worldwide.

Global financial crises and the market crash in 2008, when a lot of people lost their money and went into bankruptcy, made us even richer, prosperous and influential because of my successful and smart leadership. Gerald Bank posted an incredibly high profit that year. It was killing time for many, but not for us.

* * *

But lately the business is not going so well.

Two months after my birthday party I went earlier than usual to my office at the bank.

I was nervous.

I was scared.

I was about to pour a large whiskey when my secretary Florence said over the intercom:

"The gentlemen are here for the meeting at nine. Do you want me to invite them into the boardroom?"

I looked at the clock on the wall. It was approaching nine o'clock. It was a very important meeting with heads of departments. I went to the boardroom.

"Come in gentlemen," Florence said.

The men took their places around the conference table. I opened the meeting, confident as usual, with a cold, haughty voice. They looked at me with respect. None of them noticed my nervousness and my efforts to hide how scared I was.

"Gentlemen, the reason I asked you to come today is not very pleasant. Several recent potential deals have failed and I'm assuming that there is someone who is disclosing confidential information. The most recent case was yesterday when the offer for millions in the high-tech sector wasn't accepted. You are the heads of our departments and therefore I demand that you be especially attentive. I will give an additional bonus to everyone who helps me find the reason."

"Any specific information?" said the head of the loans department.

"No evidence implicating someone on our staff," I answered.

"Perhaps this series of unsuccessful transactions is just coincidence," said the head of the markets and research department.

"I thought so at first, but we didn't just lose deals. Someone is taking them in the last moment. Someone internal works against us. I want everyone to be very careful."

"Do you think that last week's computer network server crash was sabotage?" asked again the head of the loans department. "Remember the chaos that day? And SWIFT stopped working."

I shrugged.

"I don't know. It's quite possible. The incidents have became too much to ignore. I have already given orders to increase the security."

"What about the cameras, Elliott?" asked the customer service manager.

"Nothing that would lead us to this person. All employees know that there are cameras and that telephone calls are recorded. So whoever is responsible is doing it outside of the bank. Well, gentlemen, thanks for coming. Have a nice day."

After the meeting, I asked my secretary to call Robert to come over.

"Someone sells information. All department heads and dispatchers were notified by protection and security. Today we will discuss all this again at the board meeting. We must be very careful."

"Do you have any idea who it might be?"

"Of course not. It's an employee of the bank or a family member. This is a man who has a good reason to come into my office. Otherwise, how else could my smart phone mysteriously disappear from my desk?"

"Disappear? I haven't heard about it," he interrupted me.

"I didn't want people to know."

"I didn't get that. Why on earth is someone stealing a mobile phone?"

"Because the thief knew that the phone contains contact information for the most important clients, and some secret codes. Its memory contained the names and telephone numbers of all firms and key figures involved in future transactions. It wasn't stolen. I got it back."

"And you think that someone took the info quickly and replaced the phone in the hope that you would not notice?"

"Maybe. I'm sure the phone was on my desk. Then I was in Florence's office for a while. When I returned to my desk the cell wasn't there. After an hour or so it was back on my desk."

"We should have minimized the number of people who had access to your office."

"Unfortunately we could not. It was the day of the press conference about the personnel changes and the budget for the football team."

"I don't want to change the topic, Elliott, but why on earth are you sponsoring this football team? You even don't like football."

"Yeah, you're right. In fact, I bought this team just for some advertising."

"Well, I still don't understand how the cell was taken."

"I told you it was a person from inside. After the press conference a lot of people came into my office - journalists, photographers, athletes. It was a perfect time to take the phone, to transfer the info on the USB and to return it. I realize that it isn't just a theft but something more."

"Maybe someone hates you personally and it has nothing to do with the bank. Have you thought about that?"

"It is possible that someone wants to clear up the old accounts, but whoever it is I'll find out."

"I'm sure that you will."

"Let's stop here with this topic. I would like you to present your action plan as Executive VP. What are your views on your responsibilities in this position? Prepare a report and give it to me as soon as possible. Any questions?"

* * *

When he left I stayed silent for a while, watching the sun playing on the floor.

I could smell the end of summer. At this time of the year the sun was already low and the sunlight was dancing playfully on the expensive exotic carpet.

Nine years I'd spent in this room and every year at this time I watched this solar tease.

How long would I have this opportunity?

I already had enough evidence to believe that someone has made me a target. I'm experienced enough to understand that behind all these dirty games is someone's hidden desire to destroy me.

Putting together the mosaic of events and facts of the past few months, I realized that this attack on me was a carefully considered action. There was no doubt that someone had decided to take my place and my power.

Of course, I had no intention to let this happen.

Who might be that jerk?

My nephew John? I couldn't prove that he was selling confidential banking information, even though I had some doubts.

My brother Oliver, who also has worked a long time for the bank? He hates me. Well, I knew he would never forgive me for the fact that he was my employee.

The children of Melanie? They were also employees of the bank, but they were very young and lacked experience. I was almost sure that Melanie had done everything possible to encourage their hostility towards me. She believes I killed our brother Ben.

But I didn't. How could I kill my own brother and make my

mother suffer?

Melanie is crazy.

Anyway, she was always very well informed about everything and especially about our conflict and struggle for the bank with Ben.

Not that it wasn't true, but if I have to be precise, he stood against me and wanted to take my place.

I acted in self-defense.

The issue was life or death - him or me.

He wanted the bank, I wanted it too. One of us had to disappear. I was really lucky that I found myself the winner of that tough match. Yes, I took some steps to eliminate him but I didn't kill him.

It was someone else. But how could I prove it? And again I returned to the previous question: could I have complete confidence and trust in John, Ben's son, and was he as attached to me as he seemed?

I thought the answer was "no."

His promotion was his test.

* * *

I had a conversation with my brother Oliver after John came to work in the bank.

"For me personally, Elliott, you made a mistake taking John into the bank since you once had problems with his father."

"I didn't kill his father."

"I?m not saying that you killed him but you had a conflict with him. A reasonable person would understand the logic of the arguments I have put forward, but not someone like you, Elliott."

"You're wrong," I told him. "I care enough for Ben's family, so John loves me and he will be grateful. You are just scared too much, Oliver. That's all."

"I don't know how such a pragmatic and brutal man like you, Elliott, can be so stupidly naive. To trust such an employee is just dangerous."

I replied then:

"You're so funny."

"It's not funny. And yes, I'm scared. I can admit it without any shame that this young man awakens in my heart a constant fear of retaliation or physical retribution."

"Ha, ha, ha. Are you serious?"

"Listen, Elliott. I'm not even joking. There were oddities in his behavior, which are scary. We cannot afford to hide our heads in the sand any longer."

"You really make me laugh. Go on! Let's hear everything."

"Can you stop laughing? I'm serious here. John is too perfect, sterile, which is not typical for a man of his generation and his age. It's exactly this neatness that frightens and worries me. He apparently has no vices - no drinking, no smoking, he's not a womanizer. Our nephew is truly a young gentleman - reserved, but polite and helpful to all."

"I cannot see anything bad in this."

"I wonder, though: is this real? It seemed to me that this excellence is directed and intentional. But I'm not sure what his motivation is, although I have some suspicion."

"Really?" I said ironically.

My brother looked mad at me.

"Look at him, man. He is dressed in an elegant and expensive but conservative style that suits me and you, not him. Always immaculate appearance. It smells of something fake, my friend"

"I like his style. He not only looks good but also he works very hard. He works in the bank until late at night and on weekends. This constancy in his efforts to improve has made him an out-and-out professional, well informed, competent, with a definite contribution of attracting new clients. I like all of that."

"I like all that too. But the question here is not what we all like. My question here is why he wants us to like him so much? Don't you understand, Elliott? How to express myself more clearly? He is too perfect to be plausible."

I interrupted him:

"Why not? I know a couple of people that are exactly like him. Do you want me to give you an example?"

"Maybe I'm too guilty or suspicious, but I cannot suppress my hunch that he schemes to trap us."

"But you have to." I said softly.

"You need to trust me."

"I truly do." I said softly again.

"I don't think so, Elliott. I don't think so."

"I don't really understand your problem, Oliver. Anyway your son refused to work in the bank."

"It is not about my son at all. It is about the success of the family business. We are here to work for the better future of the whole family. If I can see that someone can cause troubles, my duty is to tell you that."

"John is from this family too."

"Sometimes it's not enough to be a member of the family, to fight for the family interests."

We had a couple of conversations on that topic.

All of them with the same result.

That is to say - no result.

Actually I was wrong. There was a result. John became the new vice president of the Gerald bank.

* * *

Anyway, my brothers Ted and Ben were *dead.*

Did someone kill them?

I have a serious reason to suspect that someone did.

Maybe I was the next target.

I'm scared to admit it even to myself, but the truth is that I no longer have close to me such a high class person as Ted. A person whom I can trust. A man with a strong mind and at the same time so susceptible to my influence.

I missed him so much.

* * *

My brothers and I grew up together and they were aware of all my childhood youth pranks and high school secrets.

As students at Harvard we led pretty charmed lives, our nights were endless parties, alcohol and girls. But we jealously kept this to ourselves so it was not known by our family. I was very close with my eldest brother, Ted. Subsequently he was a participant in all my schemes and financial games. He knew all the "tools" that correctly or not I used when making deals in the bank.

He didn't know, and will never understand how deftly I managed to discredit him in our father Robert's eyes, causing him to change his opinion about his eldest son.

Intentionally, I often visited our father Robert in the bank to seek advice, to talk about the affairs of the bank and my particular job. During these long talks I didn't fail to mention how much I admired him and how I wanted to be like him. I managed to convince him that I really did have a lot of his qualities - an enterprising spirit, ingenuity, ambition and devotion to family. At the same time I found ways to mention how impractical Ted was, how wrong he had reacted in one or another situation and how I wouldn't have made such a naive and simple mistake, and so on and so forth.

For years, persistently and systematically I instilled in our father the idea that Ted was a man who couldn't cope with a responsible job in company management. So when my father appointed me, I was the only one who met without surprise the news of the new head of the Gerald Corporation.

I made Ted the vice president and tried to compensate him with money and power for what I had done. But I forgot about these intentions very soon. If he dared to contradict or to impose on my opinion I had to put him in his spot. But still, he was loyal and fulfilled all my orders, even the crazy and absurd ones.

When I discovered that Ted was adopted I was shocked. He was not our blood but our father loved him more than his biological sons as he was the child of his first love Maggie. If I were to believe my grandmother that all evil is punished, I should expect deserved retribution for my devious deeds. I really did a lot to provoke God's wrath.

* * *

I moved my eyes from the sun playing on the floor.

Okay, let's face the facts - all my relatives might at any time be an enemy.

It could be Melanie!

It could be one of her children.

It could potentially be John, Oliver, Robert.

Even Pamela.

Now, for the first time, I realized I'm actually alone.

How did that happen?
I needed my family to be with me, not to oppose me.
Who was plotting against me?
I was alone.
I had only Elizabeth left.

* * *

I wanted to see her. Last night she didn't feel well and I told her to take a sick day. Well it is nearly noon so I could go. My only wish at that moment was to be with her. As though she were my only safe harbor in this sea of lies and betrayal.

Before going out I called Pamela.

The butler said that my wife had gone out.

"When?" I asked, puzzled. At that time Pamela usually watched her daytime TV shows.

"About an hour ago," said Maxim in his soft Russian accent.

I put the phone down, wondering where she could be, but after a few moments I had already forgotten about her.

I told my secretary to cancel my lunch appointment with a client who owed me a favour. Florence looked at me surprised, as it was rare for me to cancel business meetings. She hid her astonishment behind her usual phrase:

"Yes, sir."

CHAPTER THREE

I rushed towards Elizabeth's place followed by my body guard, who was right behind me like an invisible shadow. The weather was nice and warm. The streets were crowded with people. Most of the women were dressed in light and airy dresses making their curvy bodies look sexy and voluptuous. While scanning their alluring figures I somehow unconsciously stepped up my pace so as to be with Elizabeth sooner.

I stopped at the corner to buy for her some flowers and candy.

I tried to open the door with my key but it was locked inside. Elizabeth opened the door after I had been ringing a couple of times. She was wearing light green pajamas.

My beloved one didn't look happy to see me and didn't even try to hide it. Elizabeth was the last to conceal her real feelings. Hypocrisy wasn't one of her traits.

"Elliott? What are you doing here in the middle of the day?" she said angrily.

"You are not delighted to see me, are you?" I asked, not hiding my disappointment.

"Definitely not. I'm feeling disgusting. I don't want to see people right now."

"Even me?"

"I said: anyone."

"Damn! I have canceled a few business meetings so I could see you. I bought you flowers, something I do rarely, and you don't even allow me to come in."

"I didn't ask you to do so."

"And what do you suggest to do with these flowers? To throw them out the window?"

"God, no! Give the flowers to me. Thanks for the candy as well. I didn't want to offend you, but I'm not feeling well. You should call me before coming."

"Maybe you want me to hire a secretary for you, so I can call her and make an appointment to visit you?"

"Listen," she said in an angry mood, "I am grateful for every-thing you did for me - the promotion, this apartment. Maybe you think that after giving me all this luxury that you have bought me?"

"I don't think that…" I tried to say but she yelled:

"Then why are you treating me as if I'm property or a toy that you can use just to have fun?"

"Elizabeth…."

"Isn't it clear that I'm not a thing you can buy. I have value, of course, but there is no man who can afford it. In this sense I'm priceless. I'm not your property, Elliott Gerald, and never will be so…."

This woman was driving me crazy.

I said angrily:

"Stop it. I've never perceived you as an object."

"Then I want you to consider my opinion and my desires."

"Well, you think I'm not doing this?" I asked as I gazed at her.

I couldn't understand her and never would.

She behaved sometimes like an angel, giving me paradise, or as a sinner, ready to take me to the hell.

She could be a passionate and experienced seductress, then a shy innocent girl.

She was completely unpredictable and I never knew whether she would fly into my arms with a loving kiss or would scream that she hates me to death.

"No, you're not doing this," she answered my question. "Today is a perfect example of how you treat me."

"After all this I better leave," I said.

She was still mad at me and said:

"I want you to coordinate our meetings in the future. I don't think you would be happy if I rushed into your office and said I wanted to do it on your desk."

"Why? I would like the idea. But maybe it's really better to go back to the bank and leave you to have a rest." I said disappointed and ready to leave.

All of a sudden she changed her mind and said politely.

"Well, now that you are here you better stay."

I hesitated for a moment and accepted the offer, scared she

would change her mind again.

"Okay. So, we both agree that I'll stay. Now, I propose to discuss lunch because I'm dying of hunger," I said.

She stopped me saying:

"I didn't go shopping. My refrigerator is empty."

"I'll hire a woman for the household to do cleaning, cooking, shopping. So I'll be sure someone is taking care of you so that one day you don't die of starvation."

Elizabeth smiled.

"Obviously you miss your daughter. I don't want to be the one on which you transfer your fatherly care. Moreover, I don't want somebody to take care of me. I love my freedom."

"But it would be more comfortable for you."

"I told you I want to be alone. I don't need a housekeeper, cleaner, or anything else. I like to be alone and to take care of myself."

"Well, well, if there is no food I will call a nearby restaurant where the food is good and they provide excellent service."

"Tell them to be fast as I just realized I was hungry like a wolf."

"Okay, baby."

"Please order enough food, because I intend to spend a long and tiring afternoon with you." Elizabeth murmured in my ear and kissed me gently on the cheek while I was giving the order over the phone.

"Look at you." I smiled for the first time. "How suddenly things turned in my favor."

After about fifteen minutes two waiters appeared at the door. They quickly arranged the dining room table and asked whether we wanted service throughout lunch. I hesitated, but seeing the meaningful glances Elizabeth was giving me, I said:

"No thanks. Leave the dishes on the table for serving, please. We will call when we are finished. Thank you very much."

"Yes. Of course. Good appetite."

"We don't know when we will get to dessert, right?" Elizabeth said playfully while the waiters went out.

And she was right, because it was after five when I called them back.

The waiter came and removed the dishes and then we went to

take a shower.

"Do you know what I want to do now," said Elizabeth when we emerged from the bathroom and stretch on the bed wrapped in warm towels.

"I have no idea, but it should be something really weird...ha-ha."

So it was....

"I want to go to the multiplex, buy a large popcorn and watch one of those stupid scary movies."

"I hate that kind of movie. How can you like them?"

"Why not? We can have diner after in the restaurant nearby or go to the Macalister club where a great new band is playing."

"What if there are paparazzi?"

"So what?"

"Okay, okay, but we'll take a taxi. I have clean clothes here, right? However, I can't go with this expensive suit and tie."

"I'll give you something casual, but I don't understand why you put so much importance on stuff like clothes."

I called my bodyguard and freed him for the evening. At that moment I thought that if that bastard my invisible enemy wanted to kill me, he could come in the multiplex and empty the gun.

In the theatre, we were surrounded by a crowd of noisy youths, dressed casually, with hair formed by gel, some with bright locks of hair on their heads.

Hardly any of them would recognize me. How could they know that this casually dressed man is one of the most influential and wealthy men in America?

If I asked them: "Do you know who Elliott Gerald is?" they surely would have told me that they'd never heard of him. Who is he? An actor or a rock singer? And if, by chance they did know me, they would think "What is that senior citizen doing with this sexy young girl?" Also they would probably think about the power of money in our world.

CHAPTER FOUR

"**I** called you at lunch time," I told Pamela when I got home at nine. "Maxim told me that you were out."

"It was my Spanish course," she told me with the tone she usually uses when she announces that she is going to watch her next TV show.

"You're studying Spanish?" I stared at her in amazement.

"Yes. I enrolled in a course."

"You didn't mention that you have such intentions."

"I wanted to, but I have had no chance to talk to you. I don't even know when you will get home. You are always busy in the office or at the foundation, or at a business dinner at the golf club or somewhere else."

"I have heard about these commitments already. They are not new, but you could always find time to tell me important things."

"I don't think this course is something so important, I just decided to listen to your advice and take up a useful activity."

"And decided to study Spanish?"

"Why not? I love the Latino."

"Do you have any other ideas that I don't know about?"

"Nothing that is important for you."

"No yet?"

"Well, I became a member of the Amazon ladies' club. I go there almost every afternoon. Felicity Willow included me in their bridge team."

"Do you play bridge? Seriously? I cannot believe that. What about your TV shows?"

"Felicity's secretary records them on a USB. We'll watch them together sometimes."

"You've changed a lot lately," I muttered, but she ignored me. Then, somehow off-topic, she attacks me with a question:

"Can you intervene for a protege of Melinda Berg? The protege wants to be accepted at your golf club."

Barely concealing my amazement at the sudden change in the

conversation, I asked:

"First, tell me who he is?"

"Daniel Presley, owner of several prospering Internet companies."

"Yes. I've heard about this young man, but I don't think I could
recommend him with a clean conscience."

"Why not? Melinda said that money isn't a problem for him."

"Perhaps so, but money is not enough to get into our club."

"Really? I thought that's what was most important."

"Look, I don't trust people like Daniel Presley. He may have
money, but he lacks image and respect. I cannot accept businessmen of his type - walking into his office in shorts, with long hair,
listening to rap on his phone and thinking he is doing business."

"Are you old fashioned? What does it matter how he goes to
work if he earns tens of thousands per day? Melinda told me that
when you were his age it took you a year to earn what he earns in
a day."

"Times have changed a lot since then. These kids make fast
and good money, but it still doesn't mean they will be accepted by
serious businessmen."

"Listen, I don't argue. I just promised Melinda I'd ask you and
I want you to do it for me."

Yes, Pamela had changed. It was quite obvious. Earlier she
would never talk to me with such a sharp tone or force me to do a
favour for someone that I didn't want to. What was the reason for
the change? Was she going crazy again or was it something else?

"Listen, Pamela. I have real problems at work. Someone is tar-
geting me and I think I'm in real danger."

"Who could it be? And why?"

"I don't know. I don't trust anybody. A lot of lies and dirty
games are involved as well as a lot of money."

"Oh, stop it, please. I don't think only money is involved. All
that has happened or will happen in the future is your fault. For
your mistress you are ready to sacrifice everything - your work and
even me. You are doing things for her that you never did for me."

"Wait. What are you talking about?"

"Usually I express myself very simply saying what I have to
say, hoping that you are smart enough to understand what I mean.

Now, excuse me, but one of my shows is just starting. To be honest I prefer to watch it in my room alone."

She turned sharply and pushed the bottom of the house elevator.

"Please, don't leave me alone right now. How you can watch a movie when we have such a serious problem to solve? Just stay with me."

"I'm sorry that I'm not supportive enough, but I prefer watching movies rather than wasting my time in useless talks. Anyway, you will receive what you deserve."

I felt a note of satisfaction in her voice.

What else would a self-respecting man in my situation do but pour a large glass of scotch. After this crazy day I didn't have any desire to watch TV or listen to my favourite music. I closed my eyes and tried not to think about anything.

Suddenly I heard a familiar and insipid melody. It was Pamela's mobile phone on the table. I found nothing wrong with answering her phone.

"I would like to speak to Mrs. Gerald, please. Or maybe I have the wrong number," said a young male voice hesitantly.

"It's her husband. She is kind of busy right now."

"Hello, Mr. Gerald. Please, tell her that our workout will be tomorrow at ten o'clock in the morning, not as we agreed at late afternoon. I apologize but I can't make it at that time."

"And who is speaking?"

"Oh, sorry, I'm her personal trainer."

"Pardon?"

"My name is J.D. and I'm Mrs. Gerald's fitness coach. Please tell her that she will need to be at the gym at ten o'clock sharp... thank you."

"I'll tell her. Thanks for calling."

"Have a nice evening, Mr. Gerald and thank you, again."

I went to Pamela's room. She was lying in bed, eating from a huge bowl filled to the brim with fruit salad and watching a movie on the biggest TV screen that you could imagine, the latest model from Sony, available to very few people in this city.

When renovating the house, she wanted to combine two of the guest rooms to make a room spacious and comfortable enough to resemble a real movie theater. A room with some extras including a soft and wide bed, trays full of fruit, a drinks bar, and a special phone located next to the bed with a direct line to the kitchen and servants room.

She subsequently converted my closet into a library, storing countless USBs. Then she had me extend the south wing so that our two apartments now occupied the entire second floor of the house.

"Your coach just called," I informed her using my polite voice.

"Did he confirm the afternoon appointment? When should I be there?" she asked without taking her eyes from the TV.

"He said he can't make it in the afternoon, you need to be there at 10 a.m. Where exactly do you train, if it's not a secret? I'm asking simply because a fitness center is available here with a gym and swimming pool."

"I need someone to guide me," she swallowed a large white grape.

"Then why doesn't he come here?"

"Because I don't want him to come here. Sorry, Elliott, but I'm watching a movie...."

"I don't want to be annoying, but when did you decide to do fitness, having never stepped foot in our gym?"

"Since one morning I remembered that soon I will turn forty. Then it occurred to me that my life is passing away without me being aware of what it's about."

"And you think fitness will give you the answer to all these questions?"

"It's not just fitness; it is a new way of life. Elliott, once again, let me see the movie."

"Sorry for interrupting," I said as I got up and walked toward the door. "The issues that I tried to discuss tonight are really serious, but it seems that this soap opera is more important for you."

The commercial stated and she turned to me.

"These TV series are saying very simple truths about life, if you want to know. They are not as complicated as your banking transactions. They affect people directly and educate them about a number of virtues. These simple things are important for people, don't you think? You need to see at least one romantic movie from time to time, I am not telling you to watch a whole series, just one movie."

"Oh, no! For God's sake! I don't need such intense therapy. I live my own life and it is real. It is becoming increasingly difficult lately."

"Give me my cell back," she said as she certainly didn't hear my last words, nor heard the bitterness in it. "If you like, leave it on my bedside table. Oh, please don't pick up my phone next time. I prefer that people leave me a message."

"Do you have any secrets from me?"

"Oh, Elliott, please."

I left the cell on her table and went to my room. I called Robert's apartment, but Lucy wasn't at home. I was calling her on her mobile during the day, but it was turned off. I decided to try again, but only reached the operators expressionless voice.

* * *

The next day I woke up as usual at seven o'clock.

I woke up with a strange and oppressive feeling. I tried to remove it and started my regular morning routine of half an hour in the pool, then the usual complex exercises in the gym and a glass of freshly squeezed orange juice. While I was taking a shower I was thinking about Pamela. She has never stepped into our gym, and has not even dipped her feet in the pool. Now she visits the gym of one J.D. I would not be surprised if she also trains in a pool somewhere else. Does she do it to be far away from home?

I thought to ask her more questions, to find out more details about her new pursuits at breakfast at eight, but she didn't show up. Her personal maid said that she was still sleeping.

After breakfast, I went to the staff room to tell the driver to prepare the car to depart in thirty minutes. I had not done this for years.

"Good morning, Antonio." I told the young Mexican who drives her. "Are you going somewhere today?"

"Yes, sir. Last night senora Gerald ordered that the car be ready at nine. That's in thirty minutes."

"Mui Bien, Antonio," I muttered awkwardly and went quickly, sensing their puzzled looks.

Something strange had happened recently with Pamela. What could it be? Intuition told me that something was wrong.

While going to the office, I rang again to Lucy. Oh...a miracle! Finally I heard Lucy on the handset instead of the indifferent voice of the operator.

"Lucy, where were you all day yesterday? I tried in vain to get a hold of you. I called you on your cell and even several times on your home phone. What will it cost you to call your father from time to time?"

"Sorry, papa, but I was at a casting."

"Pardon?"

"You will not believe it, but I was offered a serious offer by the fashion house Escada. Negotiations are almost completed, I'm in the agency now fine-tuning the last details."

"I wanted to see you and talk about it."

"Sorry, papa, but I am very busy right now."

"If you still want me to help you, or just to listen to you, do not hesitate to call me."

"Sure, papa"

"Lucy?"

"Yes?"

"I'm worried about you, about your future."

"Don't worry about me. I'll be happy because I believe that new challenges wait for me."

Good God!

"Papa, here comes my agent, I cannot talk anymore I gotta go!"

I decided to play my last trump card.

"Wait a second, I wish, however, to see you at the earliest opportunity. You should know some things."

I'll call you later."

CHAPTER FIVE

I had a meeting with Red Sheep, one of my "associates" in the Petroff Corporation at noon. He sold me information about a very profitable project that had yet to be publicized. Later in the day, Red demanded that we see each other again. He had more news about the deal.

Our meeting was at an expensive and luxurious restaurant where we could speak calmly and the food was excellent.

During my long years in business I realized that business meetings of this kind need two things: the security and anonymity of the informer and fine dining.

As host, I arrived a few minutes earlier.

Red Sheep appeared at the appointed time, accurate to the minute. He was a plump, short man around fifty, with a pleasant face and glasses with metal frames.

We greeted each other like old friends because we'd known and worked together for years. He was selling me information; I was paying for it duly.

I'd been sitting at a table for two by the window when the waiter appeared.

"What will we start with?" he asked. I turned to my guest.

"Can I have Chintsano, soda and ice, please," he said.

"For me a martini."

The waiter brought the drinks quickly. I ate the olive and took a sip from the cocktail. He did the same with his Chintsano.

"How are your wife and children?" I asked. I knew from experience that an aperitif is more enjoyable with a polite and absolutely meaningless conversation.

He also knew the drill.

"They are doing well. Thanks. I hope everything is fine as well with your family. Give Pamela and your daughter my special regards."

"We are okay. Thanks, I will give them your regards." I answered him politely, knowing that he is not interested in my family; we were just following the rules of the game.

The waiter appeared.

"Will the selections remain as you ordered when you came in, Mr. Gerald," he asked politely.

"Yes, please."

When we were finishing our drinks, another waiter appeared with a cart to serve lunch.

"This is one of the best restaurants I have ever attended," said my guest when he saw a plate full of beef and a garnish of steamed, fragrant tasty vegetables.

"And the wine it just amazing," I said, while the boy poured it into our cups. "I ordered a red wine from Southern France. Do you mind?"

"No, you have made a great choice," he said and started eating with an appetite.

Once we finished the main dish we were served bowls of fruit salad covered with ice balls.

"Elliott, you spoil me."

"Yes, this is a good excuse to pamper myself.'"

Finishing our lunch, we exchanged a few more pieces of small talk such as where and how we will spend the weekend and how helpful it is to relax from time to time.

After the waiter served the coffee and left the table, I went to the point - the reason for the lunch.

"How is everything going? Are you ready to finalize the deal, yet? Or is there something happening that is disturbing?"

"I'm afraid you're right. You know…it's for big money and it is logical others would have an interest in an investment with such a return. In a nutshell, we got an offer from an investment consortium, which apparently has decided to firmly invest in the project," he slowly sipped his coffee.

"You think they are trying to undercut our numbers?"

"I don't think. I'm sure. I saw the parameters. They are better than yours. I suspect that behind this offer is dirty Russian money. Money to be laundered. I don't know, I don't like this, especially with regard to the offshore registration."

"What is the name of the consortium?"

"SRT consulting. We don't know much about them. We are

researching now. I'll let you know when there's something in particular. So, in short, Elliott, things are no longer as sure as they looked like in the beginning. And that is the fault of the spy in your office. Apparently they knew everything."

I took a sip of coffee while my mind worked quickly. My face remained expressionless. Clearly, everything has come into place. Somebody worked against me at the bank. But who could it be?

"I'll pay you handsomely for any additional information you can give me about this possible competitor. This deal should be mine."

"I will do everything possible. You know I'm on your side."

"We must not allow them to grab this deal from under our noses. We must act fast to prepare a backup offer. When do you think you will have additional information?"

"Not later than a week, I hope."

"And how long should it take to decide on tenders and to start negotiations with the investors?"

"Listen, you know that thanks to me, your offer was considered as the best. Right up until this consortium's offer. I think if you try to eliminate them in some way, we will be able to sign a preliminary contract within a few days. Otherwise with the new players, things can drag on for up to a month."

"I hope we'll succeed. I'll go into my office and urge my people to act as quickly as they can on the second offer."

"Okay. But I would suggest you to find and eliminate the spy."

He finished his coffee.

"I have to go. Thanks for the wonderful lunch, Elliott. I'll call you as soon as I have more information."

We shook hands and Red Sheep went away, trying to move quickly, but his weight prevented him from doing so. So this is the way I'd remember him - trying to go fast, but actually moving slowly and clumsily.

I finished my coffee thinking about how I should act under the new circumstances.

Then I gave my gold credit card to the waiter.

CHAPTER SIX

On my way to the office I was frantically pondering my further actions.

The most important thing was to win the deal.

The team responsible for the optimization of the parameters and final completion of the revised offer would work in complete isolation and secrecy. I hired these independent experts as soon as the official bid was prepared and presented to the Petroff Corporation. Nobody knows about them, and they are working in a small office outside the bank. Of course, their silence and discretion is paid for generously.

I decided to act in this way immediately after the first failure of Robert's people. Then they missed a golden deal precisely because they had no alternatives to counter the competition. Now I had to alert these unknown experts and revise the deadline for completion of their work.

So far, so good.

What can I do with John?

Rethinking Sheep's words I became instinctively more cautious. Deep down in my mind I had already decided to check the loyalty of my nephew. I would bait a trap. So with one bullet I will hit two birds. You are a real fox, Elliott, my old friend.

* * *

"I was in preliminary discussions to implement the project for the gasification of torn areas of the central routes," I told John after I asked him to come in my office, "I got information that the main competitor will be an investment consortium named SRT Consulting. I want you and your people to gather all possible information about this consortium, including registrations, owners, origin of money, referrals, access to capital markets and so on. This is only part of the information I need. Your task will be to collect information discretely about the bosses of the consortium and their families - hobbies and habits, vices and weaknesses. Everyone has his Achilles heel, right? You'll want to consider the ways in which we could discredit any of them."

"Okay, Elliott," John said with an inherent respectful tone. "Everything will be done as you want."

The next evening, John called me on my cell phone and told me that he already knew a lot of details about the consortium, but needed one more day.

"Act fast. All this had to be on my desk yesterday."

"Sorry, Elliott, but this information is difficult to gather, the offshore registration is a puzzle. You know this."

"We have sufficient funds for such cases, so hurry up and buy what I need."

"Yes, Elliott."

"Anything else?"

"Do you have a minute?"

"Only if it is about something really significant."

"An idea. One potential deal."

"I'm always open for new ideas. Speak up."

"I've mentioned this deal before, but now I have all the information."

"Which one exactly? Remind me."

"The two hosts of Manhattan. Requesting funding for their computer program called 'From host to host."

"So?"

"I already have the final numbers, and if you have time I can show them to you tomorrow."

"Is there a good return?"

"If the project gets approved I will prepare an aggressive campaign for the product."

"I completely trust you. Tell the law department that we have approved it and to prepare the necessary documents. Finally, make sure the complete report about the deal is on my desk."

"Thank you for your trust, Elliott."

"I am glad that you are proactive. You have good instincts about these things. Keep me posted on this one."

In reality I didn't care about this project at all, my real goal was to manipulate him into thinking he has my trust so I could keep an eye on him without suspicion.

* * *

The next day he called me.

"Elliott, I know who is behind all this. Consortium. Bla, bla, bla. Behind this name hides a single offshore company. I just don't know how if it was engaged in other investment projects, how no one knew about this? You would not believe who is the majority owner."

"Really? And who is he?"

"Your friend Jason."

"Jason?"

"Yes. Jason Fearbank. The company is one hundred percent owned by him. Well, there is a fictitious share of his bank, but it is possible to throw some dust in the eyes of other shareholders. Otherwise the company is an ideal vehicle to spin free funds of the bank and to deal profitable transactions. Naturally the bulk of profit is for him."

"This son of a bitch. Listen, keep on researching."

"I think you know what his weaknesses are better than anyone. Another issue is whether in this situation you will go up against him. You know what I mean?"

"I know."

"From another source, I know that Jason has had an affair with a married woman, but no one knows who she was. If you want to continue working on the issue, I think I can figure out who she is and why Jason has so carefully protected her identity. I will try to provide conclusive evidence about who she is. But if you don't agree to extortion, I will stop here."

I pondered deeply. This blow below the belt from Jason was unexpected. Wait ...so the "mole" couldn't be Robert. He hates Jason . Robert would rather be allied with the devil.

My eyes stopped on the innocent face of John. As much as I didn't want it to be true, my suspicion was directed toward him or his people. On the other hand the offer was submitted in the last moment and only Robert knew its full and final parameters. Calm down, Elliott, everything will come into place. When I get my hands on him, Jason will tell me everything.

"Find her!"

"Okay, Elliott."

* * *

He delivered his report in person two days later. He was embarrassed and avoided my eyes.

"Elliott, I don't know how to tell you this. About Jason and his...."

"You mean his mistress."

"Yes, but...."

"Too much to worry about my friendship with Jason. Remember that this is a business and it's a lot of money at stake.

"Here it is," he handed me the report.

"Let's go into the boardroom. The video wall there is large enough for this purpose."

John was fidgeting.

"Come see the video with me."

"I have an urgent appointment."

"That can wait for a couple of minutes. Florence, I'm busy."

"Elliott...."

"Let's go and have fun."

"Elliott, believe me, it's better to watch it alone."

"Sit down, sit down and have fun."

A private detective was able to shoot a short video of Jason and a mysterious woman in his bedroom. But the light was too dim so we needed to watch the entire show and still we couldn't see her face.

"The film is quite hot," was my comment. "With these hot scenes we can make good money if we sell the copyright."

"Yes," John answered quietly.

"I'm looking forward to seeing her, and whose wife she is. I'm sorry, I probably look like a kid, but I'm having fun because I can imagine what will happen to his business."

"I don't know."

"I would like to see the expression on her husband's face if he could only see her," I continued to titter as the show moved into

the most turbulent phase. "Wow! Wow! How about this performance, John?"

A few minutes later the camera showed the enamored couple
on the partly illuminated threshold of the house. The party was
apparently finished, and they dressed and were ready to go. When
she turned to kiss Jason, her face was clearly visible in the street
light.

I was dumb with surprise.

It was Pamela....

I don't know how long I stood petrified when I heard John
saying:

"I'm sorry, Elliott."

"You had seen the video, right?"

"I needed to be sure that it would work. As you ordered, I
hired a private detective to follow Jason and take pictures of the
couple. I was no less shocked than you when I recognized Pamela,
believe me. I wanted to let you watch yourself, but you insisted
that I stay."

"Damn.! Dirty bitch! Doing it with one of my best friends."

"I'm really sorry. I was thinking what to do after watching the
video, even thought to destroy the record. Finally I decided that
despite that it would be painful for you, it is better to know the
truth."

"You did the right thing. Thank you."

"Can I do something to help you?"

"No, no one can help a man who is a cuckold."

"Elliott, I...."

"Leave me alone, please, and once again thank you."

He left, quietly.

My cell phone rang. I went to the desk and picked it up.

There was no ID on the display. I thought it might be Lucy,
and was about to dial her number when my eyes stopped on a
large yellow envelope that someone had left prominently on my
desk.

I opened it slowly and suspiciously because Florence didn't
tell me about any incoming documents. Maybe John had brought
it. Subconsciously I expected to discover new shit and it was really so.

From the inside of the envelope poured negatives and photos fit for a pornographic publication. They clearly showed the bodies of Jason and Pamela.

I threw it on the floor. I started to choke, cough, I couldn't breathe. I was having a panic attack. I had experienced such crises before but surely this would be the worst in my life. I thought that my end was coming.

CHAPTER SEVEN

When **I got home,** Pamela was watching her show and didn't pay any attention to me.

"Did everyone succeed in exchanging their sexual partners?"

"Pardon?"

"I was just wondering how the romantic relationships are going on." My voice was completely calm.

"I don't want to offend you, Elliott, but I don't like your irony."

She stood up and went to the bar and began to load the coffee maker. This was her new obsession - a special variety of coffee that energizes the body. She doesn't permit anyone else to prepare it for her.

"Will you give me some coffee?"

She looked at me surprised, because I never drank coffee at that time.

"If you want," and put a cup in front of me.

"Are there some changes in our relationship?"

"What do you mean?"

"Do you have a lover?"

She looked at me suspiciously to see if I'd learned something, or was just guessing. She paused and then said hesitantly:

"No. Why?"

"I expected to hear the truth."

"I told you the truth," but her voice sounded uncertain.

"Another lie and I feel my anger will boil over before the coffee maker."

"Why would I lie to you?" she didn't give up.

"I warned you not to do it."

"Elliott what's wrong with you, I...." she mechanically took the jug of coffee to pour into the glasses.

"Spare me the explanations. I'll be direct. I know that you have a relationship with another man. I just wanted to hear your confession."

She poured the coffee.

"Stop playing hide and seek. I want to hear his name."

She understood that I knew.

"Jason Fearbank," she said without looking at me.

She knew me well enough and knew that if I'd learned the existence of her affair, I'd also know the man's name.

I knew the name, of course, but I didn't expect that it would hurt me so deeply when I heard it from her lips.

I drank the coffee mechanically. The hot liquid burned my tongue. I spit it back into the glass and started coughing painfully.

Pamela looked at me startled. She probably thought I was having another attack.

"Why?"

"Because I need a man. For you it is better to thrust into your lover's bed every night, right? The arrogance here is that you brought her to the party at home."

"Wait, wait for a moment."

But I couldn't stop her. Her long suppressed discontent erupted like a volcano.

"I waited long enough. Recall our understanding about our right to privacy."

"I am not talking about that." I tried again to interrupt the flow of words, but again unsuccessfully.

Suddenly, I could see her aging. Her face was contorted in anger but I could see wrinkles hidden by expensive cosmetics.

"I will not let you to manipulate me anymore. I don't have time to wait. I realized that life flows as the sea and sand between my fingers and...."

"Would you stop?" I yelled when she stopped to catch a breath. Why him, why this aging playboy? Could you not find another decent man? Don't you think a little bit for me? Don't you realize how I feel about your relationship with my friend?"

"Because he is such a womanizer, I can offer myself without a shred of shame and I knew he would not mind to include me on his list," she whispered softly. "I was afraid that anyone else would tell the story to the tabloid press."

"This is so disgusting."

"I don't think so. Don't look at me with that haughty face. It was you who started it all."

"I didn't do it with your friend."

"What is the problem here who he or she is and whether we know them or not. And is the fact that I don't know your mistress make your cheating with her less disgusting? What about your promise not to fall in love and to stop your relationship?"

She took a deep breath and continued:

"I saw enough on your birthday. To me you're head over ears in love. I can read it on your face."

"I don't know how it got this way. Maybe in your soaps it is very romantic to cheat with a friend of your husband, but it deeply disgusts me. Just the thought that you were in Jason's bed drives me mad. Or maybe you invited him in my bed?"

"I have my own bed."

"I cannot believe his. You invited him home to your bed? But surely you forget that this house is mine too. Don't you dare lie to me! Tell me! Did Jason come here?"

I knew that when pressed, Pamela would not dare to lie to me. Now I eagerly waited for her reply. As I thought she did not hide, but I was not prepared to hear it. Still hoping for another answer, she said slowly and coldly:

"A few times only."

"I just refuse to believe it. In my house!"

"And you brought her into my home!"

"But I never took her to bed."

"And what's the difference?"

Suddenly the truth hit me:

"So, while I was with Elizabeth you were with Jason at home? To get revenge against me. You probably thought that it would be terribly exciting for you? How silent is Jason in bed? Probably much louder than me?"

"Don't be cynical for God's sake. You know very well that Jason gave me what I needed, was vital to me and gave me what you couldn't."

"Let's stop going around in this vicious circle. I learned every-thing I needed to know. Oh, one more question. When did this affair start?"

"I convinced Jason at your foundation event."

"That's why you insisted on coming to the exhibition. I was

wondering...."

"I didn't care about your charity games. I knew I would see him there."

I got up and walked quickly toward the door.

"Where are you going?"

"I have to settle some things."

"With Jason? Don't do this, he isn't guilty at all. I started the affair." She jumped up, caught me and grabbed my hand to stop me. "I almost forced him."

"You forced him. What does that mean? Maybe we should accept this as a favour and a friendly service?"

"No."

"I know how long it takes a woman to force Jason to jump into her bed...no more than a minute."

"Wait, please. What do you want? A scandal?"

"Why didn't you think about our reputation earlier? Why didn't you tell me about your relationship with Jason? Why did I have to learn about it in the most ugly and humiliating way?"

"Who told you?"

"Oh, you're finally asking me. It should have been your first question. I learned it from a lousy video and a series of erotic, not to say pornographic, pictures that John brought to my office."

"John? What has he got to do with this?"

"John was doing investigation on my order. A private detective shot a short movie."

"Don't tell me that you ordered John to hire someone to follow me?"

"Nothing like that. You weren't the object of our observation. But imagine how I felt when John and I were watching your performance in Jason's bedroom. You should know that after that I experienced the worst panic attack of my life."

"John was watching me?"

"Yeah!"

"Oh!"

She was pale as a marble and slumped on the couch.

"If you had shared everything with me, we wouldn't be in this stupid situation now. Thank you for that loyalty. Now I cannot do anything to stop the gossips."

She was silent. Then slow and trembling said:

"Wait, if I heard right I was not the object of your observation. So you've been following Jason. Why?"

"This doesn't concern you."

"I want to know. Tell me! Why?"

"I told you, this is not your business."

"Yes, it is. I'm going to call and warn him!"

"Again, thank you for your loyalty."

"But it is cowardly. You're trying to say you're more honorable than me, but you aren't. How can you do all this to your friend?"

"Don't bother to warn Jason, because now I will go see him and he will get what he deserves. Don't you dare call him."

"I don't see how you can stop me."

"I can. Believe me, don't try. But if you do...the first thing that I will do is prevent you from having anything to do with the bank. And that will be only the beginning."

"You are a monster. How did I not understand that after all these years?"

"The world around us is full of monsters," I said. "Sometimes they are disguised as loyal wives and faithful friends. People can easily be deceived and aren't able to distinguish angels from devils."

"I have never expected that you would play your dirty games against me. I am not only disappointed. I am disgusted."

"The same here."

"You leave my room, you nasty bastard, now," her voice was thin and gaunt.

"With pleasure, pretty lady."

As I walked toward the door I felt all the hatred that Pamela had for me. At that moment I could hardly believe that this woman was my wife of eighteen years.

I left angry, called my driver and told him: "Drive to Jason's house."

Suddenly I remembered that Jason might be having dinner outside as he usually did and called him on his cell.

We hadn't seen each other for several months and not since the last meeting for the governing council of the Gerald Art Foundation. Years ago Jason and I became personally committed to the cause of this foundation. It supports young talents. Even then, Jason warmly embraced the idea of patronage and was always actively participating in the work of the Foundation. I now knew the reason why Jason had not called me.

"Hi, it's Elliott," I said when he finally picked up the phone. I could hear very clearly the voices of a lot of people around him.

"Elliott?"

"I want to see you," I got to the point without giving him an opportunity to think too much.

"Oh, very nice, haven't seen you for a long time. May I know if there is some special occasion," his voice was trying to be calm but I could hear the hidden tension.

"Business," my answer was laconic.

"Is it very urgent?"

"It's not extremely urgent, but it is better to get the job done as quickly as possible."

"Maybe tomorrow?"

"No, we need to talk now."

"Well, I'm currently at a pub. I'll give you the address."

"Probably you are not alone?"

"I'm not. She's beautiful, but as you know not so smart," he laughed with his habitual cynicism. "Don't worry about her."

"It is a private conversation."

"You increasingly intrigue me."

"I'm driving to your house now. I'll wait for you there. How long will it take you to come?"

"Ten minutes max. I'm close to my house."

"Okay. See you there."

"If you arrive before me, tell the doorman that I'm expecting you and enter."

But the porter let me go in without any problems.

His home was sumptuously furnished, with deliberate luxury and ostentation which was typical of Jason himself. The unique living room connects with all other areas of the main floor. Up the stairs among bedrooms and guest rooms was the bedroom, which he considers to be the landmark of his home.

* * *

The women were his weakness *from the earliest boyhood when we were in the same class in high school. This weakness pursued him into adulthood and probably will follow him to the grave.*

Several times he tried to seduce even my secretary Florence.

One day I became an unwitting witness of one of these attempts. Jason was coming to see me regarding a business deal. On leaving he had forgotten his sunglasses. I saw them on the small coffee table and decided to catch up and hand them back.

I walked into the secretary's office. He was watching her with an expression that said he wanted to eat her. The soft, thick carpet muffled my steps and they didn't hear me. He was standing with his back towards me, and thus completely hid me from Florence's view.

"You look great as always, baby," he said.

"Thank you," she replied politely and tried to continue working on her computer.

I was about to say he forgot his glasses when he said:

"I'm sick of watching pretty girls like you fade in the company of uninteresting types like Elliott Gerald."

"Mr. Fearbank, please." Florence said and tried to print a document on the printer.

"Believe me, dear. Elliott knows nothing about women and is boring as death. But now we both could have great fun. How about an intimate dinner in Brother Peter? For example, tomorrow night? After the dinner we will go to my house and I will show you my collection of paintings. We will also listen...."

"Thanks, but I don't accept such invitations," the voice of Florence was still polite.

Every time when Jason would say: "Lord, what a woman." I would explain that Florence was not a spoon for his mouth. "You have no chance with her; don't waste your time," I explicitly warned him.

But he did not give up.

"Maybe you need the company of a real man, baby."

"I will find him myself," I felt that Florence began to lose patience.

I decided to intervene and resolve the problem, but at this moment Jason grabbed Florence in a predatory way and kissed her. For a moment she stood surprised, but somehow managed to escape from his grip and

161

stood up abruptly. Then she slapped him with such unsuspected force that his head nearly rattled the wall. Jason, struck dumb with wonder, grabbed his burning cheek.

I didn't know what would have followed if I hadn't burst into loud laughter.

"I see you don't need my help, Florence," I kept laughing. While in a state of embarrassment she straightened her disheveled hair and her shirt.

"Sorry, Mr. Gerald," she said and I saw her face flushed with shame.

"If anyone should be sorry it is not you, it's that bully. Grab your sunglasses, Jason, and get out of here because I'm really mad of you. You're just an animal."

"Well, don't take it so seriously, man. I was just joking."

"Get out."

"You don't even know what you are missing, baby," he turned to Florence before he left.

* * *

This story could be considered *as harmless child's play compared to what he had caused to Ted. Years ago, Jason consciously and ruthlessly took Ted's fiancee and defiled their old friendship forever. Their wedding was to take place just one month later, but he seduced the girl who Ted loved madly. Then he secretly went with her to Europe on a romantic trip. Before boarding the flight Jason was pleased to call and tell me about this adventure. The little coward did not even have the courage to call Ted. That's why I got the honor of telling him the truth. I had never seen an abandoned man suffer so greatly for the loss of a false woman.*

In late summer Jason returned to New York, he was already in the company of another woman - a young and naive girl who he had met in Venice. There, he abandoned Ted's beloved one and accompanied by his new acquisition returned home.

"Don't blame me for anything," he said. "It is not my fault and I don't feel guilty at all for Ted's suffering. She willingly followed me to Europe. So my conscience is clean and my sleep is completely calm."

Ted somehow survived this double betrayal and quickly got married to a girl working in the bank. Soon Robert was born.

Probably, Jason thought and felt the same way even now, when with-

out any scruples, he was having fun with my wife.

His former wife Roberta was the only real love in his life, if we assume he was capable of such a holy feeling.

They met in high school; she was in our history class in grade twelve. His interest in the beautiful, long-legged girl led quickly to marriage but it did not last long. Very soon after their marriage he started cheating on her. For a long time it remained hidden from his young wife. But gossip inevitably spreads.

It was exactly the time when their first child was born that she found out about his other women. Roberta decided to keep their marriage and had hoped that after the baby things would get better. But she was naive to believe that her husband would change his habits.

She was a beautiful and cute girl and things seemed to be better for a while. But who could stop Jason? Men with insatiable sexuality were punished by God. They flash from flower to flower in search of eternal change, change they need to exist.

Jason just didn't appreciate the opportunity Roberta gave him. The number of his amorous adventures kept growing. Finally Roberta took her child and left him. They lived separately for a few months. Jason often visited them and urged his wife to give him a last chance. He promised to stop cheating and somehow managed to persuade Roberta to come back home.

After nine months their second daughter, Judy, was born. They were a happy family for a while but not for a long time.

This is what happened. The scenario was repeated, just like Hollywood dramas. Less than one year after the second baby was born Roberta left him forever.

While claiming that he missed his family, deep inside Jason was pleased that he'd regained his freedom. He just wasn't designed for such a life. Since officially splitting with her husband, Roberta went to live in Santa Monica with her parents.

This has completely untied Jason's hands and he turned his huge house into a real brothel. The furnished castle became his love nest. When we gathered there for parties he behaved like a real kid. Loudly and without any shame he was telling us different stories about his lovers. For me this seemed like a real illness.

* * *

Unfortunately, among these bitches was my own wife. I wasn't prepared to hear his "expertise" about her. "How many times has she come here?" I looked around as if I would hear the answer from the beautiful furniture that may still have the smell of Pamela's perfume. But suddenly some noise interrupted my thoughts. Jason came in, attached to a young and beautiful girl, about the age of his daughters.

Maybe Pamela was right in telling me that she forced him to start their relationship.

Obviously he felt instinctively that we were going to have a difficult conversation because he came into the living room alone. Jason was in his early fifties but still attractive. I've known him for very long time, since our childhood, and the Fearbanks are considered our extended family. Tonight, for the first time in our long, long friendship I looked at him with new eyes, not as a friend but as a rival. It wasn't difficult to see why women were crazy about him. 1.80m tall, big and strong. Black, sparkling eyes, pepper-and-salt hair that was neatly styled, and a charming smile. He was the George Clooney of Wall Street. "Women like me not because of my appearance but because of my intelligence. I don't carry a lot of sex appeal," he used to say to us. At that time I didn't pay any attention to his words as I didn't care about his stories. Staying in front of him today I could say with very strong confidence that he was wrong. Jason Fearbank was one of the sexiest man I have ever met.

He looked at me sharply, trying to understand what my mood was, but my face was completely expressionless.

"Elliott, I'm so glad to see you." he told me in a voice that sounded very relaxed but really wasn't. He wasn't able to hide the rising anxiety from showing on his face.

Was he afraid?

"I can't believe you did this to me." I decided to get straight to the point. Concern was clearly written on his face.

"What are you talking about? You said this is about business?"

"Yes. It is. I want to make a deal for a deal with you."

"Okay." he was visibly relieved. "What is this all about, man?"

"It may be a little complicated for you, but I have some things I'm sure you will want to own."

"What do you mean?"

"It's about these pictures. Open the envelope and see for your-self."

I handed it over without stopping to watch him.

He obediently took out the contents and looked at them. His face turned to stone.

"How did you get that?"

"Oh! I have also a video with the same content. Good memories?"

"Good memories? Why you are doing this?"

"These are the family problems which don't relate to you, but I guess you wouldn't want to see these pictures in the tabloids?"

"Wait, I don't understand, you're blackmailing me? With your own wife? There is no logic, or maybe it's something really important to you."

"Yes, it is because I want you to stop your bid with the Petroff Corporation."

"You know about my participation in the project?"

"Yes. Tell me who is your informant at the bank? Do not beat around the bush and try to gain time. Just give me a name."

"I received your bid information from my staff. Someone sent it to my assistant."

"And what my friend, you didn't hesitate to try and outsmart me?"

"You know...nothing personal. This is just business."

"So, to summarize, I'm losing millions of dollars and you are sleeping with my wife. Do you think I'll forgive you for all this?"

"Oh, don't talk about morality, please. If you were me you would do the same."

"I didn't come here to argue with you. I'm here to set out my conditions."

"Otherwise?"

"Otherwise, I will give the pictures to the media. It would be a good reason to file for divorce from Pamela."

"Go ahead. I don't care. What do I have to lose?"

"Don't be so sure. You will be compromised in the industry forever. You know how these conservative people look at a man who is betraying his best friend."

"Come on...this is not serious. I'm neither the first nor will I be the last to do such a thing. And people know me and my weakness."

"Let's think together. Imagine what a spectacle it will be. I will draw out the divorce proceedings for as long as possible. My lawyers will go for moral damages. I'm sure there will be a huge scandal in yellow newspapers for months ahead. You will be compromised and thrown out of the industry forever, believe me."

"And you are able to bring all this onto your wife?"

"Be sure of that. She did everything possible to lose my trust and loyalty."

"Elliott, I understand very well that this story with Pamela is just a convenient excuse to knock me out of the deal. I know the whole truth about your relationship. Pamela just came to me one day, desperate and lonely."

"And you decided to comfort her?"

"To be honest, you should be doing that not me."

"Are you saying that you are doing me a favor by sleeping with my wife?"

"I don't understand what your problem is. After all you have your mistress?"

"Yes, but I properly notified her who the woman was. She simply didn't give me the same honesty."

"Pamela told me about your affair but I didn't believe her. It sounded so ridiculous even to me."

"You two are the people who allowed this absurdity to happen. Pamela's fault is that out of thousands of men she chose you. Why? Perhaps you were the most easily accessible?"

"Ask her, but I don't see what the difference is between me or any other."

"The difference is huge, but I don't expect an asshole like you to understand it."

"Why are you doing all of this, Elliott?"

"I don't have to give you any explanations. I have set clear conditions. You are accepting them, or...."

"Or what?"

"Or I call my lawyers and the show begins."

"Well...obviously I'm nobler than you. We'll withdraw from

the deal, although it's a lot of money."

"You don't care about Pamela at all, but only for yourself. Actually I don't care. I want you to act immediately."

"Pardon?"

"You heard me right. You'll immediately order your team to cancel the offer and to take back all supporting documents. And don't try to outsmart me again, because tomorrow it will be reported to me."

"I'll do it, please leave my home now."

"I'm not moving even a step out of here until I hear with my own ears, you talking with your boys...set up the phone on speaker please. I want to hear your voices clearly."

He looked at me with hatred, but he did obey. After he finished the conversation I gave him the negatives and said calmly:

"The original tape is in my safe. I'll send it tomorrow by courier after I'm convinced that everything is okay. You have my word that I didn't make copies."

It was all over. From then on, we were enemies. Along the way, I decided to spend the night with Elizabeth, and when I came out on the lighted street, I hurriedly pulled out my cell phone.

CHAPTER EIGHT

When **I went to my office the next day,** I received the
expected message from Red. The text was simple: "the meeting
with Mr. Eddie will not take place because he has refused."

Everything was going according the plan. I called Florence
and when she appeared at the door I said quickly:

"Please, send this package to Mr.Fearbank."

So far so good. I could expect a call from the Petroff
Corporation in a few days.

There are days in which everything goes well.

In the late afternoon I got a call from Petroff Corporation.
Their representative said there was no problem signing a preliminary contract and to start negotiations on finalizing the investment
deal. I told John to notify the legal department and to form a team
to start the procedure.

The day was very successful for me. I got what I wanted so I
decided to go home and to finish another difficult deal...with
Pamela.

* * *

She was at her usual place in front of the TV. Her face was
tense. Apparently even her favorite drama series couldn't take her
away from her worries. Still in pajamas, apparently she spent the
day in bed. She looked just exhausted.

"It was a wise thing that you didn't call our mutual friend." I
said sarcastically. "It was a complete surprise."

"How is he?" she whispered.

"Oh, calm down, dear. Last night I left him in the company of
a girl who is the same age as his daughter. The only thing we
should worry about is how he survived this night. You know,
nothing fatal, however we are becoming old."

She looked at me puzzled.

"You mean...you didn't...."

"You think I killed him? Oh, Pamela. You're just extremely old-fashioned. Who fights for women nowadays?"

She turned to me. She looked awful. Her hair was hanging upside down like a bundle of wet seaweed. Her face without any makeup seemed quite old.

"So...is he well?"

"Did you hear what I said? I left him in the arms of a desperately young bitch who probably took his health during the night. I didn't even touch him. Well, except the fact that he had to lose some money."

"What have you done?"

"Actually we did a small deal, but otherwise he was safe and sound."

"Deal? Deal with what?"

"I made an agreement with your lover that compromising materials should disappear. He paid $20 million. I could feel his pain when he did that, but all the wining cards were in my hands."

"Are you saying that you blackmailed him into paying you $20 million for the video?"

"He didn't pay me. He just lost this money."

"You won another dirty deal, didn't you?"

"The dirtiest deal...yeah."

"I'm sure you will keep the originals, right?"

"Of course. It depends entirely on the behavior of the two of you if I will use them."

If her eyes could kill, I'd already be dead....

"You're the most disgusting and vile human being I know."

* * *

Over the next several weeks things arranged themselves in the best possible ways for me while I concentrated on my work in the bank. The contract with the Petroff Corporation was signed and the investment project started. This deal will be very profitable for the bank.

Jason was keeping silent.

So was Pamela.

I had put them both on the spot.

* * *

I concentrated on my work in the bank.

The head of the human resources department came into my office.

"I have enough evidence that Paul Grisham from loans is not loyal to the bank."

"It's enough to fire him immediately."

"Yes, Mr. Gerald. I just want to remind you that his dismissal could bring us trouble with the unions."

"I want to see his dismissal on my desk tomorrow."

"Yes, Mr. Gerald."

"Cynthia Johnson has issued statements that undermine the bank's prestige. All employees have signed confidentiality agreements, agreements that state they will not comment expressly to the press on what they see or hear about the bank, right?"

"Yes, that is right, Mr. Gerald."

"If Ms. Johnson fails to comply, she should be dismissed. I'll think about whether or not to sue for damages caused."

"Mrs. Little John from the analyses department is to be sent on courses to improve her skills. The bank will pay all related expenses. We need to foster employee loyalty."

I want my staff to know that I'm well informed and appreciate and will reward their hard work and loyalty. A substantial monthly prize for the best bank employee was established. After its implementation, the head of human resources reported that this incentive was received very well. So I arranged a monthly video conference meeting to introduce a similar incentive in branches of the Gerald Bank throughout the country. These measures helped to achieve a certain balance in the relationship between management and employees.

That was only part of the work that was done.

The security systems were modernized. More security guards were hired.

Everything and everyone was under surveillance control.

I did everything that needed to be done to protect myself but I knew that it was not over.

My invisible enemy was still there.

He wouldn't give up until he received what he wanted.
If it is necessary he will kill me.

To be continued

Don't miss *Wet affairs* book two of the Geralds saga trilogy

www.ingramcontent.com/pod-product-compliance
Lightning Source LLC
Chambersburg PA
CBHW071533040426
42452CB00008B/1003